PENGUI

TILL TALAQ ᴅᴏ ᴜꜱ ᴘᴀʀᴛ

Ziya Us Salam is an associate editor with *Frontline*. A noted literary and social commentator, he is involved in building bridges of commonality through a study of the Vedas and the Quran.

He has served on the jury of the International Film Festival of India (IFFI) and been a part of the jury for Best Writing on Cinema in 2008. He has also been on the preview committee of IFFI (world cinema). His book *Delhi 4 Shows: Talkies of Yesteryear*, a study based on the cinema halls of Delhi, was released in 2016. In 2012, he edited a book titled *Housefull: The Golden Age of Hindi Cinema*.

Adopting a multilayered approach, he writes about literary and cinematic developments regularly and has contributed to anthologies published by the publications division of the ministry of information and broadcasting and the British Council, among others.

His book *Of Saffron Flags and Skull Caps* will be out soon.

ADVANCE PRAISE FOR *TILL TALAQ DO US PART*

'This book delves deep into the forms of divorce sanctioned by the Quran, of which there are nine, including mutual consent, available to both husband and wife. Triple talaq is not sanctioned by Islam and has already been banned in many Muslim countries'

—Nayantara Sahgal, author

'Ziya Us Salam's timely book explains all you need to know about triple talaq . . . It is an important contribution to our understanding of what the process of divorce is according to Islam. A must-read for those interested in gender, community and Islam'

—Zoya Hasan, professor emerita,
Jawaharlal Nehru University

'*Till Talaq Do Us Part* by Ziya Us Salam is a fine effort to meticulously and logically put together relevant matter in the context related to talaq in Islam, the viewpoints of different schools of thought, practices followed by various sections of the Muslim society, legal developments around it in India and opinions of legal experts.

'Despite disagreements on various observations, [I believe] the book will be very helpful for those who wish to understand the need and the spirit behind the provision of talaq in Islam. It will also be helpful to give an exposure [to the] social system of Islam, its true spirit and the rationale behind it'

—Mohammad Salim Engineer,
secretary general, Jamaat-e-Islami Hind

till

talaq

do us

part

Understanding Talaq, Triple Talaq and Khula

ZIYA US SALAM

Foreword by **Faizan Mustafa**
Vice chancellor, NALSAR University of Law

PENGUIN BOOKS

An imprint of Penguin Random House

PENGUIN BOOKS

USA | Canada | UK | Ireland | Australia
New Zealand | India | South Africa | China

Penguin Books is part of the Penguin Random House group of companies
whose addresses can be found at global.penguinrandomhouse.com

Published by Penguin Random House India Pvt. Ltd
7th Floor, Infinity Tower C, DLF Cyber City,
Gurgaon 122 002, Haryana, India

Penguin
Random House
India

First published in Penguin Books by Penguin Random House India 2018

ISBN 9780143442509

Typeset in Aldine401 BT by Manipal Digital Systems, Manipal
Printed at Replika Press Pvt. Ltd, India

www.penguin.co.in

MIX
Paper from
responsible sources
FSC® C016779

To Uzma Ausaf,
my biwi, *my anchor*

Contents

Foreword

The Muslim Personal Law is nothing but an 'opinion of jurists' and therefore, strictly speaking, it is not 'law' within the ambit of Article 13(3) of the Constitution of India. We need not look at the Quran to find the law governing a particular school of Islam. Ideally, we should examine the juristic opinion of the school concerned. Moreover, since Article 26 protects freedom of religion of even a 'sect', we cannot impose the law of one sect over another. In the past, the ulema would freely adopt the rules of other schools. The Dissolution of Muslim Marriage Act, 1939, was passed at the instance of the Hanafi ulema who adopted the Maliki law. Why they refused to adopt the more rational position of other schools or follow the liberal opinion of their own jurists on the issue of triple divorce is not clear. Their failure has contributed to the current crises.

Juristic opinion on the validity of triple talaq is indeed divided. The author has rightly quoted the Quran which declares in Surah Baqarah, verses 229 and 230, that 'Divorce can be pronounced twice: then, either honourable retention or kind release should follow . . . Then, if he divorces her, she shall not be lawful to him unless she first takes another for a husband.'

The expression 'al-talaqu marratan' in verse 229 means that divorce may be pronounced twice. Marratan (twice) implies a gap between two pronouncements, which would mean there should be sufficient gap between two pronouncements of divorce. When we say, 'I went to your office twice but you were not there', it cannot mean that you went to the office twice in one go. It means you went once and then again after a reasonable period of time. Similarly, there has to be a gap between the divorces, and thus instant triple divorce in one sentence or three sentences in one sitting is indeed against the Quran.

Imam Bukhari considers triple divorce as being valid from the above verse and emphasizes the words 'if he divorces her', which refer to the third time. Most Sunni schools, except Ahl-e-Hadith, consider triple divorce valid.

Some jurists are of the view that the Prophet's face turned red on hearing about the pronouncement of triple divorce—he stood up and is believed to have said, 'You have made a mockery of the Quran in my lifetime.' On the basis of this Hadith, some hold that triple divorce in one go is not valid. Others argue that had divorce not become effective, the Prophet would not have been so angry.

But Sahih Muslim and Abu Da'ud (two authentic collections of Hadiths) tell us that during the Prophet's life, during Abu Bakr's period and for the first two years of Umar's caliphate, three divorces given at a time were treated as one divorce. During Caliph Umar's time, many men would divorce their wives. Later, when the cooling-off period would be about to end, they would take back the divorce. They would then repeat the act. To put an end to this mockery, the caliph approved of three divorces in one sitting, but he took the wife's opinion too. The divorce was solemnized if the woman, too, agreed to it. The man was then subjected to lashes as a punishment for instant divorce.

Thus, though the dominant juristic view did hold triple divorce in one sitting as valid, there were enough dissenting voices in each school of Islam which considered three pronouncements in one go as just one revocable pronouncement. At least after the Supreme Court's judgment, the Indian ulema should consider adopting this alternative view and clearly declare that three divorces in one go would be counted as one pronouncement. People, too, adopt or discard juristic views as per their convenience.

Indeed, the incidence of triple divorce is low. In some cases, even when divorce is mutual or at the instance of the wife after the failure of several rounds of arbitration, mediators and lawyers themselves advise parties to record triple divorce because they think three pronouncements must be made or recorded in writing. As per Census 2011, only 0.49 per cent Muslim women were divorcees, and all of them had not been given triple divorce. The Quran itself lays down an elaborate procedure of divorce, which has now been accepted by the All India Muslim Personal

Law Board. The Muslim women who had gone to court were basically demanding nothing more than just reverting to the procedure of divorce mentioned in the Quran.

Under the Quranic scheme now adopted by the board, if there are differences between the spouses, they should amicably try to resolve them by talking to each other in the spirit of forgiveness. If this does not yield the desired results, there may follow a temporary withdrawal while they continue to live in the same house. If the first two steps fail, and if differences continue to persist, the two parties should try sincere reconciliation by turning to their families or by appointing an arbiter from each side, who would leave no stone unturned to help the spouses reconcile. If arbitration does not yield positive results and there is no possibility of a patch-up, with irretrievable breakdown of the marriage clear, only one divorce is to be pronounced by the husband. This single pronouncement is to be compulsorily followed by a waiting period of three months, or, if the wife is pregnant, till the child is born. If during this waiting period the spouses change their mind and want to stay married, the divorce stands revoked. Lastly, if no revocation takes place within the waiting period, divorce is considered to be complete at the end of three months or the extended period due to pregnancy. Thus, only one divorce is enough to dissolve a Muslim marriage.

In my opinion, the government should make a *nikahnama* compulsory, which explicitly states that were a marriage to end, instant triple divorce will not be considered an option. Such conditions were routinely included in the nikahnamas drafted during the Mughal rule. My esteemed teacher and eminent historian Prof. Shireen Moosvi has reproduced several such nikahnamas. Criminal sanctions must be used as a 'last resort', when all other means cannot give the desired results.

Ziya Us Salam's book on triple divorce is timely and will help us understand the intricate issues related to it. He has rightly and boldly demonstrated that while triple divorce gets a lot of public and media attention, other forms of divorce available to both Muslim men and women are hardly spoken about. He has exposed the biased reporting of triple divorce by quoting one example where a husband divorced his wife in a graveyard. No report on this divorce mentioned the vital fact that this couple was in fact living in the graveyard. Even Shayara Bano's husband moved the court for restitution of conjugal rights, and therefore wanted to save his marriage. The author rightly says that divorce in Islam is not like 'two-minute noodles'. He has also given details of his conversation with several clerics, some of whom told him that they do treat three divorces as one revocable pronouncement.

The book will be of great use for those who want to get a quick grasp over the subject. All those who want to speak, write about or understand the controversial subject of triple divorce will find this book not only handy and readable but also immensely useful.

Faizan Mustafa
Vice Chancellor,
NALSAR University of Law, Hyderabad

Introduction

On 22 August 2017, India exhaled collectively! Instant triple talaq, or talaq pronounced in a single sitting, was declared invalid by the Supreme Court. In a landmark judgment, the five-judge bench comprising the then chief justice of India J.S. Khehar, Justice Kurian Joseph, Justice R.F. Nariman, Justice U.U. Lalit and Justice S. Abdul Nazeer, through a split 3–2 verdict, set aside instant triple talaq. Hearing the plea issued during the *Shayara Bano vs the Union of India and Others* case, the judges termed it arbitrary and in violation of Muslim women's right to equality. Justice Joseph, whose vote proved decisive in setting aside instant triple talaq, came up with a memorable statement:

> What is held to be bad in the Holy Quran cannot be good in Shariat and, in that sense, what is bad in theology is bad in law as well . . . Merely because a practice has continued for long, that by itself cannot make it valid if it has been expressly declared to be impermissible.

The next day, this judgment occupied prime space on the front page of all English, Hindi, Urdu and regional dailies. Leading newspapers like *The Hindu*, *Times of India*, *Hindustan Times*, *Indian Express* and *Tribune* opened their editions with bold headlines. 'Instant talaq: Unlawful, unlawful, unlawful' screamed *Times of India*. *Hindustan Times* was not far behind with its forthright headline, 'No, no, no: Triple Talaq is declared illegal by SC'. *Indian Express*'s New Delhi edition was more adventurous. Its bold, black headline 'Talaq, Talaq, Talaq' had a red line cutting right across it. The impact was all in the visuals. *The Hindu* was predictably more sober and straightforward with its headline 'No, no, no: SC on instant triple talaq'. *Tribune* too restricted itself to 'Instant triple talaq banned'. Urdu dailies like the *Rashtriya Sahara* and *Inquilab* used bold fonts to announce the Supreme Court's decision.

Such was the frenzy over the much-awaited judgment—Chief Justice Khehar was retiring in less than a week—that the Doklam standoff was treated almost as a footnote by most newspapers, with some failing to find space for it on their opening page! Talaq occupied all the space and attention. In most newspapers, there were multiple stories on page one, followed by more analytical pieces with expert comments inside. Though it occupied reams and reams of space, the expanse of coverage given to instant triple talaq was neither new nor unexpected. At one level, it sent the mind racing back to 1982, when noted film director B.R. Chopra's *Nikaah* was released. The film, starring Pakistani actress Salma Agha, had melodious music by Ravi and a memorable ghazal by Ghulam Ali. Yet, it made bigger news—in fact, an uproar—for all the wrong reasons. The film centred on a case of instant triple talaq, in which the hero packs his wife off by uttering the three dreaded words. That there was no prior attempt at reconciliation, or even a witness to the talaq, mattered not in the least. The Hindi film industry has never been particular about details. In this case, however, the shocking lack of attention to the process of talaq in Islam caused such an uproar that not only were hoardings of the film blackened by some women activists, but police protection had to be provided at some cinema halls screening the film in Madhya Pradesh, Uttar Pradesh and Maharashtra. In Delhi, many burqa-clad women gheraoed the popular Golcha cinema in the first couple of weeks—though they later came back to enjoy the film many times over. The media then, like the media in 2017, concentrated on the surface; the details were too time-consuming and involved too much research and study. The Urdu newspapers, never known for being ahead of the times, were full of debates around triple talaq in which the slant, more often than not, favoured it! 'It was a sinful but effective way of divorce,' they often surmised in 1982. This did not change a bit in 2017.

Back then, the highly regarded Urdu daily *Al Jamiat*, brought out by Jamiat Ulema-e-Hind—incidentally, one of the parties to the Shayara Bano case in the Supreme Court—had carried in-depth stories on the subject of divorce. It had even opened its otherwise sacrosanct editorial page to outside clerics. *Dawat*, a daily brought out by the Jamaat-e-Islami Hind on recycled paper, stayed away from even a mention of the film, concentrating instead on the process of divorce in the Quran. Yet, none of the newspapers talked in any detail about khula or *talaq-e-tafweez* (where the husband vests the power of divorce with the wife), the focus invariably being on *talaq-e-biddat* (called an innovated form of divorce), 'a sinful but effective way of divorce'! Quoted often in defence of instant talaq was a purported ruling of Caliph Umar. Only rarely was Prophet Muhammad's stance on the subject referred to in detail. It may be recalled that once, when a man came to him admitting to have given three divorces at one time to his wife, the Prophet regarded it as a single, revocable divorce, and gave the man the option of going back to his wife. Beyond the Quranic verses dealing explicitly with talaq—Surah Baqarah, Surah Nisa and Surah Talaq—hardly any attention was given to Surah Ahzab, which talked of *zihar*, another form of divorce beyond the talaq. And not once did an alim, a commentator, think it wise to tell the community that the men were expected to refrain from using instant triple talaq simply because they could not go against the Sunna of the Prophet.

The slant of the other newspapers was clearly different. Here, the attempt was not so much to find the truth behind the much-talked-about way of divorce, but to create an impression of 'hapless Muslim women at the whims and fancies of men'. A Hindi newspaper, subtlety clearly not among its strengths, carried features on talaq for days on end, with every feature arguing against any form of divorce whatsoever. Marriage, for the newspaper, was all about seven lives! That was the merger of reel and real life in 1982.

Not much has changed in the last thirty-odd years. For the last five years or so in particular, the issue of triple talaq has often been raised in sociopolitical and media circles. Every now and then, the issue makes headlines with a tale of the agony of a woman at the receiving end of instant divorce. Almost each time, the irrational, unjustifiable action of a temperamental man is used to convey a larger picture of all Muslim women living in constant fear of divorce. That the rate of divorce in the community is among the lowest in the country, according to Census 2011, does not matter to people forever ready to jump to convenient and instant conclusions. Hardly any attempt is made to get to the bottom of the issue. Not many distinguished academics or scholars have written about the woman's right to divorce available in Islam. The media too does not bother to present the complete picture. Way back in the early 1990s, when this author wrote a piece for *Pioneer* on khula, the woman's right to divorce in Islam, it failed to get much attention. Yet, a following piece for *Patriot* on the plight of a woman who had been given instant triple talaq by her husband at a cemetery garnered much attention. The fact that the estranged couple actually lived in the *qabrastan*, or graveyard, with the man being the imam there, seemed to matter little. Just the fact that the woman was divorced in a cemetery was enough to make headlines—the underlying message being: divorce does not leave a Muslim woman even at the time of death! All this selective ignorance means that even today, in the eyes of the common man, instant triple talaq is the only way of ending a marriage in Islam. Not many bother to find out or learn about khula, talaq-e-tafweez, *lian*, *mubaraat* or zihar, etc. Worse, even Muslim men and women in metropolitan cities, supposedly better educated and with greater access to the tools of information, do not know about *talaq-e-ahsan* or *talaq-e-hasan*, the two accepted forms of talaq available to a man. Indeed, hours after the Supreme Court judgment in 2017, ignorance was yet to be lifted from the roads and lanes of the country. When *The Hindu* conducted a tour of the walled city of Delhi, most respondents were not aware of the court's verdict. And when they were apprised of it, they instantly said that they favoured the retention of instant triple talaq, calling the Supreme Court judgment 'interference' in their personal affairs. Most Muslim women were either unaware of the verdict or regarded society like a superculture, one that could ride roughshod over a Supreme Court ruling setting aside instant triple talaq.

The proof of the limitations of the verdict came from Jharkhand the next day, where a man divorced his wife using the instant triple talaq method. Twenty-seven-year-old Fatima Suraiya from Hazaribagh alleged that her husband, Faiqi Alam, had breakfast with her. In the evening, though, without any warning or hint, he divorced her through the talaq-e-biddat method! With the utterance of the three dreaded words, Suraiya and her daughter were thrown out of the house. No local cleric intervened. In fact, the *qazi*, instead of simply considering it a single, revocable divorce, after the pronouncement of which the wife could not be thrown out of the house by the husband, sought twenty days' time to arrive at a decision when Suraiya asked for help!

And to think that just a few hours before Faiqi pronounced instant triple talaq to get rid of his wife, the Supreme Court had invalidated his action! Still, this instance of instant talaq brought into focus the stark reality: the Supreme Court had merely set aside instant triple talaq. It could not have set a punishment, like the penalty of a certain amount of money or years to be spent in jail, in case a man was guilty of the use of arbitrary divorce—that falls within the domain of the legislature. To the relief of some women activists and many liberals, the government introduced the Muslim Women (Protection of Right on Marriage) Bill, 2017, which sought to imprison a man guilty of delivering instant triple talaq for three years. The Bill, however, was silent on how maintenance would be provided to a woman if her husband was in jail. It also ruled out any attempt at reconciliation, which defeated the purpose of legislation. Incidentally, the apex court had highlighted the opportunity for reconciliation as emphasized by the Quran. The Supreme Court did not state clearly if the marriage in such cases subsisted. And if it did, what was the security for a woman against a repeat divorce, maybe through a Quran-approved method the next time? The Supreme Court judges pronounced their decision in New Delhi, but in the small towns and villages of India, social norms are often paramount, all law subservient to them. That explains why both dowry and the caste system continue to prevail despite strictures against both.

Suraiya's triple talaq brought back to mind the affidavit submitted by the All India Muslim Personal Law Board in the Supreme Court, wherein the Board promised to tell the qazis who solemnize nikahs to incorporate a condition in the nikahnama that the marriage, in case of any problem, would not be dissolved through the triple talaq method. Pray, what authority can a non-statutory body in the country have when the highest court's verdict failed to awaken even women in Delhi, or dissuade a man from giving his wife instant triple talaq in Jharkhand?

A few days after Suraiya's divorce was reported in a section of the media, I stumbled upon a cleric from Bareilly in western Uttar Pradesh. The township is known for its dargahs, and what this cleric shared was pretty interesting: 'We get plenty of cases of triple talaq, and more than a handful of khula. For every case of khula, we get eight to ten cases of triple talaq. Usually, people from the lower segment, the less educated ones, come to us for help. The better educated ones can read the Quran themselves, even its commentary,' he said. 'Read the Quran, did you say?' I asked the man to double-check. 'Yes. We do the same when giving a decision in any talaq case.' So that means triple talaq is not accepted? 'No, we consider it a single divorce only. If we go into the Hadith, there are so many contradictory ones available. Everybody can quote or misquote one to suit their argument. Which ones to follow? So we just go by the Quran.' He made it sound so simple and logical.

Around 120 kilometres from Bareilly, in Kashipur, clerics presented a contradictory view to Shayara Bano's father when he consulted them about her marriage after the receipt of the *talaqnama*, with the word talaq written over it three times. They ruled that the marriage was over. Triple talaq was final, it was irrevocable. There was no way of reuniting her with her husband. Unfortunately, in the run-up to the so-called final divorce, when Shayara Bano was going through tumultuous times in her marriage with Rizwan Ahmed in Allahabad, nobody there, or later in Kashipur, told her about the options she had to walk out on a man who demanded dowry or was physically abusive. According to the law of the Quran, she was entitled to take khula and start her life all over again. It could have saved her a lot of personal anguish and public humiliation. Similarly, when Atiya Sabri was subjected to character assassination by her husband, she was within her rights to end the marriage through lian, a way of divorce wherein if the husband charges his wife with adultery and is unable to provide proof, the wife is entitled to seek divorce. Clearly, the Quran and the Sunna protect women's honour, their marriage and their rights. Society is guilty of either misinformation or, in some cases, disinformation. All of this is so contradictory and a bit confusing too, I thought.

Thus began this exercise of clearing the air around the issue of divorce in Islam. The idea was to present a complete picture with the help of the Quran and back it up with instances from the Hadith and history. It may be stated that sharia is based on the Quran and the sayings and traditions of the Prophet. Without getting too bogged down by the niceties of different schools of Sunnis—Hanafi, Shafi'i, Maliki and Hanbalis—the attempt here is to present a broad picture and help the common man understand what divorce in Islam is, how it can and should be avoided, and how it can be enforced. That common man, or woman, need not necessarily be a Muslim experiencing the crests and troughs of marriage. It can be anybody who is perplexed at the glut of images of divorce on our television screens, the reams of space in our print media, and being none the wiser for it! Yes, Islam allows a man to divorce his wife, but there is a process for it. It is not like two-minute noodles or switching off the ignition of your car. It allows a woman, too, to dissolve her marriage. It gives both men and women the right to step out of wedlock through mutual consent. How? Through these chapters, I have tried to explain what you need to know about divorce in Islam.

This book would not have been possible without my twenty-year-old association with Prof. Tahir Mahmood, as erudite a scholar of Islam as any I have met in my life. As the chairman of the National Commission for Minorities, he was often generous with his time and knowledge of the minority affairs of the country. Nothing has changed over the years—he shared his viewpoint on divorce in Islam and the lack of authenticity in the tradition of instant triple talaq. As a journalist, I have also been a beneficiary of Prof. Faizan Mustafa's vast knowledge and enviable skills at the dissection of the issue for the past two decades. That has been time well spent. His writings in

The Hindu, *Tribune* and *Indian Express* helped clear many a
cobweb. Equally important has been my relatively recent
association with Prof. A. Faizur Rahman, who has gone
over the niceties of various schools of thought with a
fine-toothed comb and was happy to share with me a bit
of his knowledge and independent thought process. He
helped me lend a perspective to the issue beyond the oft-
quoted Hadith. A vote of thanks is due to Prof. Shireen
Moosvi, whose immeasurable bank of knowledge
of medieval nikahnama came in handy. A picture of
modesty, she was generous with her time and knowledge.
As was Rohit De Sahab, a historian at Yale University. He
happily shared his insights into personal laws in many
Muslim countries. Special thanks to my father-in-law,
Dr Syed Ausaf Saied Vasfi sahab, who went through the
religious injunctions on the subject presented here to
vouch for their authenticity. Not to forget Anjana Rajan,
who took time out to read *Till Talaq Do Us Part* despite
her commitments. Of course, this book would not have
been possible without Milee Ashwarya, as unassuming
an editor as one can aspire to get. One fine afternoon, I
shared the idea of this book with her. A few days later,
she sent me a mail of acceptance for the proposal! What
followed was a series of inputs from her to improve the
content and presentation of the book.

My gratitude to all my colleagues at *The Hindu*—
Frontline, especially R. Vijayasankar, who has never been
short of a good word, and my friends John Cherian,
Venkitesh Ramakrishnan, V. Venkatesan, Purnima Tripathi,
T.K. Rajalakshmi, Divya Trivedi and Akshay Deshmane,

whose silent support and animated discussions have made *Till Talaq Do Us Part* possible. I am also grateful to Aamir Abdul Rashid sahab, brothers Abdul Azim, Iftikhar Ali Hashmi, Aftab Alam, Aslam Khan, Irfan Ahmed, Masroor Mian, Rashid Ali, Mohammed Qumar Khan and dear S.M. Umair, for their inputs at various times. Of course, a big thanks to my wife, children and sisters for being there for me, as also to my dear friends Vijay Lokapally, Anuj Kumar, S. Ravi and Madhur. A big hug to Khadim Hussain, a brother like none other, for urging me to write the book all along.

Before we end, a request to all readers: for the sake of readability, I have not used the suffix 'peace be upon him' after every mention of Prophet Muhammad's name, as is the correct way. Please do say 'peace be upon him' after taking his name. Similarly, any mention of a caliph or any of the wives of the Prophet Muhammad (peace be upon him) should be followed by the expression 'may God agree with him/her'.

1

'Like Garments unto Each Other'

Marriages may be made in heaven, but they are solemnized on earth. The Quran too assures us that there is a mate for everybody. 'And among His signs is this, that He created for you mates from among yourselves, that you may dwell in tranquillity with them, and He has put love and mercy between your hearts. Verily in that are signs for those who reflect,' says the Quran (Surah Rum, chapter 30, verse 21).

Yet, marriage in Islam is not necessarily a bond forever. It is a contract, signed in accordance with the wishes of the two parties, with everything penned down clearly along with the date, time and place. Right from the names of the spouses to their ages, current and permanent residential addresses, the testimony of an advocate and the names of a couple of witnesses—one from either side—everything is written down. The consent of the girl is essential for the nikah to be completed. Her consent is to be given in private without the presence of her family

members to avoid any parental pressure. She may choose
to nod in approval or express it in words. The girl has
the complete right to decide her mahr (loosely translated
as dower), which the husband is supposed to pay. It may
be paid through cash or kind at the time of the nikah or
later, but has to be paid for sure in case of a divorce. The
mahr amount is to be inserted into the nikahnama along
with any condition of immediate or deferred payment in
cash or kind. It carries the signatures of both the spouses.
Such is its importance that a man who cannot afford to
pay mahr in cash is advised to teach his wife the Quran,
or at least a surah if he knows it and she does not. Back
in the seventh century, the Prophet himself asked his
prospective son-in-law Ali what he had to offer in mahr
to his daughter, Fatimah. When Ali expressed his inability
to pay even a meagre amount, the Prophet reminded him
of a saddle he owned and advised him to sell it to provide
for mahr. It is a girl's right on her husband, with no third-
party interference. It should not be equated with the price
for cohabitation either.

Marriage is regarded as Sunna, part of the practice
of the Prophet. According to a Tirmidhi Hadith, a wife
completes half the faith of her husband. It says, 'When
a man marries, he has fulfilled half of the *deen*, so let
him fear Allah for the remaining half.' Further, another
Hadith says that the best of men are those who are the
best to their wives.

The Quran regards a man and woman like garments
unto each other. In other words, they are supposed to
protect and shield each other from the world. Rather

than being driven exclusively by the man, marriage is a team effort in which the wife complements her husband's efforts and vice versa. Under no circumstances does she surrender her own identity. If she wants to pursue her studies or career, the husband is strongly advised to support it. She is not supposed to change her maiden name, drop her surname to add her husband's family name or even add her husband's name to hers. This is a revolutionary expression if one considers the condition of women across the world some 1400 years ago. That was the time when men would decide whether a girl child had the right to live and female infanticide was rampant.

Yet, Islam provides room for divorce in case the differences between the couple are insurmountable. Among all the things permitted, divorce is despised the most by God. The provision of divorce was made to end genuinely unhappy marriages—later, a restriction on the number of marriages was also added to rein in men driven by lust. Divorce was regarded as being better than a lifetime of silent suffering or unending agony for one or both spouses. The belief was that if there were compatibility issues between a man and his wife, perhaps she would be more comfortable with another man, and he too would find peace with another woman. Hence, it was considered better to allow a couple to annul the marriage than for either to live a life of sighs or have an inappropriate relationship with another person.

Considering that Islam regards a husband and wife as the garments of each other, they are strongly advised to try and overcome mutual differences. At the first sign of problems, one is advised to not rush to family or friends for help. Agony uncles and aunts are to stay away. The husband and wife are supposed to try and overcome their differences by talking to each other. In fact, there is a Hadith about squabbling spouses, wherein the Prophet tells a husband to imagine his wife in a state of prayer to overcome his anger towards her. In another Hadith, a man is clearly told not to look for perfection in his wife. Rather, he is told to look for positive attributes; maybe she is good at something he doesn't necessarily pay attention to. Her strengths may be different from what her husband perceives. Hence, he is advised to look for the good in her. So important is the happiness of the spouse in Islam that a woman is told to hide extreme happiness in case her husband is sad or upset, and to hide her sorrow in case he comes home brimming with joy. The same advice is extended to the husband, the idea being to bring the partners on an equitable plane. Also, both men and women are advised against surrendering to lust. In fact, the Quran (Surah Nur, verse 30) asks men to keep their gaze lowered. It is only the next verse that asks the woman to do likewise. The attempt is to arrive at fair play and probity.

To avoid the initial hassles of marriage, family members and friends are advised not to disturb the privacy of the newly-wed couple. The man and woman are supposed to spend time with each other without disturbance. In case family members and friends want to visit them, they are advised to keep their visits brief, between the times of the

Asr and Maghrib prayers (prayers offered when the sun starts to decline and set).

If the wife so likes, she can choose to live separately from her husband's parents (or even her co-wives in case her husband has more than one wife. The co-wives may not even visit her house without permission). She is not obliged to cook and clean for them; her only duty is towards her husband. With the other members of her husband's family, she is expected to maintain a relationship of respect and cordiality, but she is within her rights to want to live in a nuclear family. In fact, the term 'housewife' is a bit of a misnomer in Islam; homemaker is more like it. Islam clearly puts the responsibility of looking after ageing parents on the son or daughter, not their respective spouses. It encourages nuclear families to give the woman of the house a sense of protection. A wife is within her rights to refuse to live with her husband's brothers, as they are not her *mehram* (somebody with whom a marital bond is not possible, like father, brother, uncles, etc.). Further, a husband is required to arrange for her comfort according to his means. It is not her responsibility to cook for him. Rather, it is the husband's job to arrange for a cook or a maid if he can afford one. If his means do not allow it, both husband and wife are supposed to share domestic responsibilities. The Prophet himself helped his wife in grinding wheat into flour and cleaning, etc. He would repair his shoes and clothes himself. Interestingly, while the wife has a right over her husband's money (according to a Hadith, a woman is permitted to take cash from her husband's pocket for food and other essential expenses), he has no right over her money. Even the mahr that he gives at the time of the nikah belongs exclusively to the woman. She may, of her own free will, decide to help her husband with his finances in case of need, but he cannot demand her money or force her into working if she is not so inclined. Khadijah, the first wife of the Prophet, was an extremely successful businesswoman who had initially hired him as her business manager. After their marriage, during extenuating circumstances, she was happy to share her riches with her husband and his companions.

A wife, however, is never allowed to share her husband's secrets or weaknesses with her family members. Be it his property, his children or even the little things he shares with her in good faith, they have to remain with her only. She is the custodian of all his words and wealth. In his absence, she is supposed to safeguard his home and hearth, his brood. She is considered the children's first teacher. Anything less is considered *amanat mein khayanat* (breach of trust). She is supposed to groom herself well for him (and vice versa) and greet him with love and care. She has to remain chaste and loyal. She has every right over him as long as she maintains this decorum.

With such clear-cut dictates, a husband and wife should be able to overcome their differences mutually. They can sit in the privacy of their bedroom to thrash out the issue or step out for a walk to come to common terms. However, in case they are unable to do so, a ready advisory is available in the form of the Quran. Rather than make a public spectacle of their suffering, they are advised to call two witnesses, one from each side, to help them. If possible, these should be the witnesses to the nikah, and preferably family members of the two parties as they are more likely to know the shortcomings in the temper or disposition of both the husband and the wife. The Quran, through Surah Nisa, verse 35, says, 'And if you fear a breach between the two, appoint an arbiter from his people and an arbiter from her people. If they both desire agreement, Allah will effect harmony between them.' Noted Islamic scholar Abdullah Yusuf Ali hailed it as a move that prevents chicanery and misuse of the law. Contemporary scholar Maulana Wahiduddin Khan, in his book *Concerning Divorce*, refers to arbiters as a third party without any vested interest: 'Not having any previous association with the matters under dispute, he [the arbitrator] will remain dispassionate and will be able to arrive at an objective decision, acceptable to both parties.'

Even at this stage of third party–moderated dialogue and discussion, the attempt is to save the marriage and provide a mutually acceptable solution to the spouses. The arbiters are not supposed to have just a one-off chat with the sparring spouses. They are supposed to interact regularly over a period of three months to find common ground—this long period usually facilitates the cooling down of tempers, enabling the couple to realize their mistakes and start afresh. The arbiters too are encouraged to help the husband and wife stay together in harmony. In fact, in Malaysia and Pakistan divorce is not possible without exploring the option of reconciliation through arbiters. According to a Hadith, a person is even allowed to speak a half-truth to bring the warring spouses together. The arbiters are supposed to help the couple bring life back on to an even keel and not disclose any ugly truths or half-truths they may stumble upon during their interaction with the couple. The marital woes of a couple should never become the talk of the town. All along, the emphasis is on justice. No party should suffer. For instance, men are told to make sure that they are able to look after a woman before mooting the idea of nikah. In case a man is not financially stable, he is advised to fast as that helps keep a lid on desire. According to a part of Surah Nur, verse 33, 'And let those who find not the financial means for marriage keep themselves chaste, until Allah enriches them of His bounty.'

Also, a man should be able to fulfil his conjugal responsibilities to the satisfaction of his wife. In case a man is impotent, he is advised against marriage. A marriage in which the man is aware of his inability to cohabit with his partner amounts to cheating. In such cases, a woman can opt for instant dissolution of marriage through khula. She is not required to give any reason or proof for the same. Also, it does not entail a period of three menstrual cycles.

Coming back to the witnesses, they are advised to keep the foibles or the shortcomings of the couple to themselves. However, even after serious arbitration and efforts to make the marriage work, they might not achieve the desired result. Yet, the conclusion the arbiters arrive at has to be honoured by both the husband and the wife. During the reign of Caliph Ali, the fourth caliph, a couple approached him for arbitration. The wife pledged to accept the decision, whichever way it went. The husband did not, whereupon the caliph is reported to have asked him to fall in line for any negotiation or settlement to take place. 'What you say is improper. By God, you cannot move from here until you have shown your willingness to accept the verdict of the arbiters in the same spirit as the woman has shown,' he said.

However, if the arbiters too feel that there is no way to return to peace and quiet, the man is allowed to opt for divorce. There is a clear process for divorce outlined by the Quran. The divorce cannot be pronounced in a drunken state. Nor can it be pronounced in a fit of rage so intense that a person becomes incoherent. If pronounced in either of these states, the divorce is invalid. Also, divorce can only be pronounced by the husband during his wife's *tuhr*. Tuhr stands for 'clean or pure condition', a time when the woman is not having her menses. It is also the period when he would not have established physical contact with her. In case the husband pronounces divorce during his wife's menses, it is automatically annulled. The rationale here is that a woman is at her most vulnerable at this time and might not be in an emotional state to tackle such a condition. The Prophet, in fact, ordered a wife to be taken back if the divorce was pronounced during her menstrual period. Of course, any promulgation of divorce has to have actual intention behind it. If, after its pronouncement, a man denies his intention, his word is accepted and the divorce stands annulled. This can be done only during the iddat period or the term of waiting.

Though there are differences of opinion between the various schools of jurisprudence, they come from recourse to certain Hadiths and laying more importance on some than on others. There is, however, unanimity on the total acceptance of the procedure of divorce outlined in the Quran. The Quran refers to different types of divorce available in Islam—not just the talaq, but others like khula, lian, zihar, etc. Its chapters titled Baqarah, Nisa, Ahzab, Mujadila and Talaq, among others, talk of various divorce options and the specific conditions in which these can be availed, besides the procedure. The options are available to both husband and wife, separately and mutually.

It is the longest chapter, Baqarah, which goes into the details. Also, the chapter titled Talaq gives clear reference points for the procedure.

Surah Baqarah's verses 226 to 237 explain the process. Verse 226 refers to those men who have taken a vow not to approach their wives for conjugal relations. It states, 'For those who take an oath of abstention from their wives, a period of four months is approved. If they return, surely, Allah is Often Forgiving, Most Merciful.'

The next verse makes divorce a possibility in such a case. It states, 'But if their intention is firm for divorce, Allah is All-Hearing, All-Knowing.' Meanwhile, women are advised not to hide their pregnancy from their husbands when divorce is pronounced. This is done to enable a husband who may have pronounced divorce without knowing about her pregnant state to take her back in matrimony.

It is the next verse of the chapter that has got maximum attention in recent times. It has often been quoted by women who approached the Supreme Court to declare instant triple talaq in one sitting invalid. The women argued that a gap of one menstrual cycle is essential between each pronouncement of divorce, and multiple pronouncements of divorce at the same time should be declared illegal. The demand was in consonance with the laws in many Muslim countries, as also the rulings of the Prophet himself. More than twenty countries consider multiple pronouncements of divorce at one time as only a single, revocable talaq. In the light of this verse, the women were within their rights to make such a demand.

A closer look at the verses from Baqarah and Talaq makes it clear that the holy book does not mention triple talaq in one sitting. Nowhere does the Quran refer to instant triple talaq or approve of it even indirectly. There is not even a hint to this effect. The book clearly reveals that talaq is allowed only when declared at appropriate intervals, on most amicable terms, through a strict procedure with terms and conditions. This, too, is possible only after all avenues of conciliation have been exhausted. Verse 229 says:

> A (statement of intent to) divorce is only permitted two times. After that, the parties should either stay together on just terms or separate with kindness. It is not lawful for you (men) to take back any of your gifts (from your wives). Except when both parties fear they would be unable to keep the limits set forth by Allah.

A simple understanding of these lines leads one to conclude that a man may divorce his wife a maximum of two times; that is, after the first pronouncement he may give a second divorce after a month. The opening words of the verse, 'al-talaqu marratan', have been interpreted to mean that divorce may be pronounced twice, with a suggested gap between each pronouncement. Arabic scholars too agree that the word marratan carries the connotation of anything done twice with a reasonable gap.

After the second divorce pronouncement, the husband and wife are supposed to live together peacefully. In case they decide to part following another pronouncement, it is to be on a note of decency and amity, with no filthy accusations hurled at each other or wrong claims made. The men are advised not to reclaim any of the gifts they may have given during happier times. They are also told to bear the expenses of child-rearing in case the divorce comes at a time when a baby needs to be suckled. A woman is required to suckle the baby for two years and the man is required to bear the cost of her food and clothing during this period. The husband and wife, after mutual consultation, may decide on a foster mother to suckle the baby. Again, the cost will have to be borne by the father.

Similarly, a simple study of verse 230 is useful in exposing the practice of *halala*. Often, in our country, cases are reported when a cleric declares that a woman has become haram for her husband after the third pronouncement of divorce, and the only way she can marry him again is if she marries another man, consummates that marriage and obtains a divorce from the new husband. Under this guise, an effort is made to procure a short-term husband, often for a night or a day or two. He is asked to marry the divorced woman and release her after consummating the marriage. The practice is against the letter and spirit of the Quran. Verse 230 states:

> And if a husband divorces his wife (a third time), then he cannot, after that, re-marry her until after she has married another husband and he has divorced her. In that case, there is no blame on either of them if they reunite, provided they feel that they can keep the limits set forth by Allah. Such are the limits set by Allah, which He makes plain for those who understand.

What this injunction means is that if a woman has been divorced for the third time by her husband, and has completed her iddat (waiting) period, she is free to marry another man of her choice. This situation is different from the first or second pronouncement of divorce. After the completion of the waiting period of the first or second divorce, the husband and wife are free to marry each other again without any third-party involvement. However, after the man has exhausted all three options of divorce, his erstwhile wife is considered a free woman. She may choose to stay single or opt for another matrimonial partner.

Now, if things do not work out with the second husband and he divorces her irrevocably, or if he dies, she will be considered a free woman again after fulfilling the iddat of her second husband. In such a position, according to this verse, the woman could marry her first husband again, provided he too were willing, and no blame would be attached to either of them.

Nowhere does this verse refer to halala as a practice where a divorced woman marries another man, experiences intimacy, obtains a divorce, then goes back to her first husband. Halala, the way it is practised in some parts of India, is a mockery of religion. It works out to be more like a short-term marriage, a modern-day *muta*, with a precondition of divorce. Any marriage with a fixed time for divorce is not valid in Islam. Marriage is a sacred bond that cannot be trifled with.

The Quran gives ample chances to a man to learn from his mistakes. In case he does not and the marriage ends in an irrevocable divorce, his erstwhile wife becomes a stranger to him. This is done to protect her honour. What this verse provides is a chance to a woman who has been divorced by her second husband, or been widowed, to go back to her first husband, as there is likely to be a greater degree of familiarity between the two. It saves her the risk of choosing another man with whom she may not have any familiarity at all. A fresh nikah is then conducted, with a new mahr amount, etc.

If the ball was in the husband's court during the iddat period after the first or second pronouncement of talaq, now the ball is in the wife's court. She may choose to marry him with all his failings, or marry anybody else, if at all.

Reading this verse along with verse 232 of the same chapter enables one to have a better understanding. Talking of divorced women, it says, 'And when you divorce women, and they fulfil the term (a waiting period of three monthly cycles), do not prevent them from marrying their former husbands, if they both agree on fair terms.'

Similarly, chapter 65, Talaq, rebuts any claims of instant talaq being permissible according to the holy book. The first two verses of the chapter unambiguously state:

O Prophet! When you (Muslims) divorce women, divorce them at their prescribed periods, and count their periods (accurately). And fear Allah, your Lord: And turn them not out of their houses, nor shall they (themselves) leave except in case they are guilty of some clear and serious (sexual) misconduct. And these are the limits set by Allah. And whosoever transgresses the set limits of Allah does indeed wrong his (own) soul. You do not know if by chance, Allah will bring about some new situation (later on). When they fulfil their appointed term, either take them back in a good (and honourable) manner. And take for witness two persons from among you, blessed with (a sense of)

justice, and establish the evidence (as if you are) before
Allah. Such is the guidance given to him who believes
in Allah and the Last Day. And for those who fear
Allah, He (always) provides a way out.

The Prophet had nine wives (though some believe it to
be eleven), but did not divorce any of them. Here, the
faithful are instructed that if they must divorce their
wives, they should do so at prescribed periods, i.e., at the
conclusion of each monthly cycle. It automatically rules
out instant divorce because neither is the condition of
attempt at reconciliation fulfilled in instances of instant
talaq, nor is the condition of counting the period of the
woman taken cognizance of.

The surah also speaks clearly of divorced women
continuing to live with their husbands during the
waiting period of three months. This is done to facilitate
reconciliation. The husband might have pronounced
divorce in a moment of haste and might regret it
upon consideration. To prevent any dire long-term
consequences for him, his wife or their children, an
option is given to annul the divorce during the iddat
period either through word or action. If, during the iddat
period, the man and woman establish physical contact,
the divorce is automatically annulled.

Also, equally importantly, the woman too is told not to
rush to her parents' or a friend's place in anguish after the
first or second pronouncement of divorce. The reasoning
is the same: if the husband and wife stay together under
the same roof, the chances of talking to each other rather

than talking at each other improve. Also, given the natural human urge, the prospects of the divorce collapsing improve significantly. All this will not be possible if the man and the woman live separately.

At the same time, to protect the wife against harassment, particularly between the first and the second pronouncements, the husband is ordered to provide for her in the same manner and style as he was before uttering talaq. And in case there is a final divorce, the women too are instructed not to have undue expectations, which the husband might not be able to fulfil. It is important to keep in mind the economic station of the husband in the whole issue. The last verse of the chapter says, 'Let the man of means spend according to his means. And the man whose resources are restricted, let him spend according to what Allah has given him. Allah puts no burden on any person beyond what He has given him. After a difficulty, Allah will soon grant relief.'

Simply put, the husband does not enjoy an unbridled right to divorce. There is a long process, involving, besides the spouses, arbiters from both families. The husband and wife have similar rights upon each other, except that the husband as the qawam (leader) is a degree superior.

3

Till Talaq Do Us Part

We hear the word 'talaq' regularly in our society. Most people think of it as an Urdu word for divorce. The word is derived from Arabic and means 'freeing or undoing the knot'. Considering marriage is a bond between a man and a woman, the term refers to divorce, as the partners are freed or the knot is undone. Islam gives a man the right to three kinds of divorce: *ila* (divorce due to vows of continence), zihar (divorce due to unnatural comparison) and the most popular, talaq.

While in the case of zihar (mentioned in Surah Ahzab) a man equates his wife with his mother, which is an unnatural comparison, in the case of ila (mentioned in verse 226 of Surah Baqarah) a husband abstains from sex with his wife for four months. Incidentally, staying away from the wife due to ill health or professional commitments, etc., does not constitute grounds for ila. It is when a man deliberately abstains from sex after pledging to do so that ila can take place.

Talaq, too, is of two kinds—*talaq-e-sunnah* and *talaq-e-biddat*. Talaq-e-sunnah carries the approval of the Prophet, whereas talaq-e-biddat is regarded as an innovated form of divorce. Further, under talaq-e-sunnah, it is possible to divorce one's wife in two ways: talaq-e-ahsan is the most preferred way of divorce and talaq-e-hasan the second most approved way. Though both practices have the approval of the Prophet, there is a fine line between them.

Under talaq-e-ahsan, the husband pronounces talaq only once during the wife's clean period, without having established physical relations. Following the pronouncement of talaq, the wife stays with the husband for the waiting period of three months. During this time, if the husband establishes physical relations with her, the divorce stands annulled. Otherwise, at the conclusion of the iddat period, the woman is free to step out and marry another man if she chooses to. Her husband cannot stop her in any way.

Talaq-e-hasan is slightly different. Here, the man pronounces one talaq only, but follows it up with another single talaq after the next menstrual cycle. If he repeats it for the third time after the next cycle, talaq is effective. The husband and wife are then a free man and woman; each may choose to do what they prefer. The Quran gives explicit instructions to not stop women from doing what they choose to do at the conclusion of the waiting period. They may choose to stay single or marry again. It is entirely their decision. Islam accepts both talaq-e-ahsan and talaq-e-hasan, but puts a restriction on two remarriages with the same man. After the first pronouncement and lapse of the iddat period following that action, the man and the woman may choose to marry each other again with a fresh nikah. The same option is available in case the woman is divorced for the second time by her husband. Then, too, the husband can establish physical relations during the iddat period and render the divorce void. If, however, the two do not come together during the three-month iddat period, they still have the option of going back to each other with a fresh nikah. This option of a fresh nikah is not available to them after the third pronouncement. Islam put a restriction on two revocable divorces because at that time in Arab society, many men were known to pronounce divorce up to ten or thirteen times. It had become a game for many; divorce a wife one month, take her back after a couple of months, repeat. Each time, the man would take back the talaq towards the end of the iddat period, and then act the same way after a while. To rid the womenfolk of this suffering, the Quran asked men to divorce women a maximum of two times, and then retain them with love and affection or part with kindness, following the third pronouncement.

Both talaq-e-ahsan and talaq-e-hasan are accepted by all countries across the world, and all Muslims, Sunnis as well as Shias, accept these as valid methods of divorce. It is, however, the third way of effecting a divorce that has divided the ulema and, indeed, the various schools of Islamic jurisprudence. Popularly called triple talaq, it is actually talaq-e-biddat, an innovated form of divorce. It is not supported by the words or spirit of the Quran. It is an instant divorce in which a man says 'I divorce you' thrice to his wife. The divorce comes into effect immediately, leaving no scope for arbitration—an essential condition which the Quran emphasizes in verse 35 of Surah Nisa. It also ignores the injunction of keeping the wife and husband together between each pronouncement to facilitate the cooling of tempers and possibly bring about reconciliation between the warring spouses.

It ignores the fact that the wordings of the Quran imply a gap between pronouncements. The Quran says, 'Divorce can be pronounced twice: then, either honourable retention or kind release should follow . . . Then, if he divorces her, she shall not be lawful to him unless she first takes another for a husband.' In Arabic, the expression 'al-talaqu marratan' implies there should be a gap between each pronouncement.

In Islamic history, the Prophet himself considered a pronouncement of talaq followed by any number as only a single, revocable divorce. There is a Sahi Muslim Hadith related by Abdullah ibn Abbas, a companion of the Prophet. He revealed that triple talaq in one sitting was considered as only a single talaq during the time of the Prophet. Things remained the same during the time of the first caliph, Abu Bakr. Indeed, in the first couple of years of Caliph Umar ibn al-Khattab's time too, a talaq followed by multiple pronouncements in one sitting was regarded as a single, revocable divorce. Even the last caliph, Ali, considered it a revocable divorce, giving the spouses some leeway to try and make their marriage work.

There is another Hadith about triple talaq being held as a single divorce by the Prophet. A man, Rukunah, pronounced three divorces on his wife but soon regretted his action. The case was brought to the Prophet, who is reported to have asked, 'How did you divorce your wife? Did you pronounce it in one sitting?' When he said yes, the Prophet said, 'Treat it as one divorce only, and if you want, you can take your wife back.' Upon his decision, Rukunah took his wife back.

In another Hadith, the Prophet is reported to have expressed his anger on the subject of instant talaq. In one such recorded instance, he is said to have stood up in anger when he got to know of a man giving triple talaq to his wife, and said, 'You have made a mockery of the Quran in my lifetime.' It was considered a pre-Islamic practice, and the Prophet remarked that its use implied the provisions of the Quran were being derided even when he was amid them.

Things changed, however, during the later years of Caliph Umar's time. When confronted with increasing instances of men divorcing their wives through instant talaq, or not treating them well during their iddat period, he said, 'Verily the people have begun to hasten in the matter in which they are required to observe respite.'

The first couple of years into Caliph Umar's time, the forces of Islam had conquered new territories, with places like Egypt, Syria and Iraq under their sway. The armed forces took many women prisoners. In some cases, they merely interacted with them and were captivated by their beauty. They wanted to marry them. In many instances, the women agreed to marry the Arab men with a precondition: they were averse to the idea of sharing their husband with a co-wife and wanted the men to divorce their existing wife/wives first. It was like an insurance they devised for themselves. Many of them believed that these men might marry them, but would ultimately go back to their earlier wives. Or even if the men gave a single divorce to their wives, they might revoke it at the end of the month or within the iddat period, leaving the new wives vulnerable. So the women prevailed upon them to pronounce irrevocable divorce on their earlier wives before marrying them. It left the men with no room to go back to their earlier wives. Many men obliged, and married the women of Syria, Iraq and Egypt. However, some of them did want to go back to their earlier wives after some time. Others were guilty of maltreating their divorced wives. It was in this light that the matter was brought before the caliph, who safeguarded the dignity of the newly married women and made triple talaq pronounced in one go as good as talaq pronounced over a period of time. It was an administrative decision meant to tackle the exigencies of the situation.

Though Caliph Umar made triple talaq valid, he put in a condition. The instant divorce would be accepted, but the man giving instant talaq would be publicly flogged. It was his way of ensuring that men desisted from the action. Any pronouncement of instant talaq was followed by the public flogging of the husband. It is this condition which modern-day maulanas have conveniently ignored, even as they declare triple talaq a valid way of divorcing one's wife.

This version of history, where Arab men were attracted to women from other places, is not accepted by scholars, who say that the caliph gave his nod to instant triple talaq for entirely different reasons. They point out that the caliph regarded three pronouncements in one go as irrevocable divorce to help women trapped in violent marriages. The women faced a danger to their lives, they contend. Also, many men used to twist the teachings of the Quran, which tells them to pronounce one divorce and then wait for at least another month before the next pronouncement. Many men would use divorce as a weapon to torment women. The scholars also agree that the ruling was for dire, exceptional circumstances.

There are other experts of Islamic law who do not agree with this interpretation of instant triple talaq. They, in fact, assert that on the contrary, the caliph never did anything which went against the letter or spirit of the Quran or the tradition of the Prophet. Among them is Tahir Mahmood, whose viewpoint on the subject was quoted before the Supreme Court by the representatives of the Bharatiya Muslim Mahila Andolan (BMMA). In his book *Muslim Law in India and Abroad*, he clearly states that the caliph's decision involved the permission of the aggrieved wife. As put forward before the honourable court:

There is no verse in the Quran that can be interpreted or stretched to mean approval of the so-called triple talaq . . . Years after the Prophet's demise, his second caliph, Umar, gave effect to triple talaq in some cases at the insistence of the wives, but after inflicting on the husband the traditional punishment of flogging. It is shocking that his action should have been treated as a binding precedent for giving effect to such an unlawful and repulsive action in every case, even against the wishes of a repentant husband and the aggrieved wife.

This decision to flog the men guilty of instant talaq, thereby discouraging the said practice, is far removed from the image of Umar often projected in Islamic history. He is said to have been the most temperamental of men, not averse to the use of violence in the early days of his life. In fact, he embraced Islam after one such instance involving his sister and the revelation of Surah Ta Ha. It is said that Umar, who had not yet embraced Islam, had set out to kill the Prophet. On the way, he met a man who was aware of his intentions and advised him to set his own house in order before trying to attack the Prophet. He was referring to Umar's sister Fatimah and her husband Sa'id ibn Zayd, who had accepted Islam. Umar is said to have gone to his sister's place immediately and found her reading from a scroll.

Scared, Fatimah tried to hide the scroll from him. Enraged, he attacked Sa'id ibn Zayd first. When Fatimah intervened to save her husband, she suffered a serious head injury. Moved by the sight of his bleeding sister, Umar asked her to show him the scroll she was reading from. On it was inscribed Surah Ta Ha, a Makkan-period chapter of the Quran that was revealed after many a batch of the faithful had migrated to Abyssinia. Upon reading it, Umar embraced Islam.

Soon, Umar rose in stature to a level where the Prophet himself is believed to have said, 'If there would have been any prophet after me, it could be Umar R.A.' Several scholars hold that many suggestions given by him were later justified by the Quranic revelation.

Interestingly, the fourth caliph, Ali, overruled the decision of Caliph Umar on triple talaq. He advised reconciliation over everything else. When confronted with the case of a couple, he set up a reconciliation committee whose findings were to be regarded as final. Today, most Islamic scholars believe that Umar's actions were for specific circumstances, and that his ruling in no way changes the word of the sharia. Nor can it be used ahead of the word of Allah, as revealed through the Quran. His decision to regard instant talaq valid was a temporary decision, but was turned into a permanent one by a section of the community. This probably gave rise to the anomaly, 'bad in theology but good in law'. The fact is that triple talaq emerged in the second Islamic century as a way for spouses to part ways when the Umayyad rulers preferred Caliph Umar's ruling ahead of the Prophet's decision as it interfered with their need for instant disposal of cases.

4

Different Schools of Sunni Thought

Far removed from the injunctions of the Quran, common Indians, including a significant section of Muslims, believe that instant talaq is the only mode of divorce available under Islam. Popularly, but erroneously, called triple talaq, this way of ending a marriage with the simple utterance of the word 'talaq' thrice has often led to an uproar in sociopolitical circles. Many human rights activists have called it an assault on the dignity of women, who are said to be vulnerable to this form of divorce despite years of wedlock. Women activists have taken umbrage at this method of divorce, which seems to give men unbridled power to end years of matrimony at the snap of a finger. It makes women vulnerable to a man's mood swings, loss of temper or burst of ego. A man might lose his temper, but the woman pays the price. While marriage is a two-way contract, instant talaq, the way it often takes shape in our society, is a unilateral action that leaves women with no scope for dialogue, arbitration or negotiation. The battle waged by the BMMA against triple talaq in the Supreme Court is merely the latest and most visible face of this struggle.

However, over the ages, even the mention of triple talaq has evoked extreme reactions. While conservative maulanas have defended it as a sinful but effective form of divorce, women in particular have been vocal against this arbitrary manner of ending a marriage. Not just in 2017–18, but since the 1970s, women have been raising their voice against instant talaq. Around the time Prime Minister Indira Gandhi imposed the Emergency in 1975, two clerics were ostracized and expelled from their cities for daring to consider triple talaq in one sitting as nothing more than a single, revocable divorce.

The first instance came from Calcutta, where Maulana Shafiur Rahman was approached by a quarrelling Bangladeshi couple. The man, Latif, had pronounced 'talaq, talaq, talaq' to his wife Hazra. Latif and Hazra had four children, all below the age of eight. Hazra was inclined to put up with his temper for the sake of the children. She herself had no support system. Her poor parents were in Bangladesh and she would have been unable to provide for the kids. She contacted a couple of imams in the city, who expressed helplessness in overruling the husband's pronouncement. The fact that there was no concept of instant talaq in Bangladesh did not help matters, as according to the local imams, the talaq was pronounced in Calcutta, so the local mores would apply.

Finally, the case was brought before Maulana Shafiur Rahman, who pronounced a brief verdict after Fajr prayers. Taking recourse to the Prophet's Sunna, wherein he considered multiple pronouncements of talaq in a single sitting as a single, revocable divorce, he declared Latif and Hazra husband and wife. The two resumed cohabitation and went on to have three more children. That did not prevent the couple from being subjected to social ridicule, with many openly asking questions about their marital status.

The maulana too was fiercely criticized by fellow clerics and the common man alike. First, he was stopped from leading the prayers as many men refused to pray behind a man who they thought did not know enough of the scriptures. Next, he was asked to leave the city as his interpretation of the scriptures had caused much dissent even among the ulema. More debate and dissent could do the community no good, it was felt.

Just a little later, Maulana Abdus Sattar was subjected to the ire of Assam's residents for trying to save the marriage of an Indian man (a local resident) and a Bangladeshi woman. Here too, following triple talaq pronounced in a fit of anger, the marriage was deemed to have ended despite the woman pleading otherwise. Sattar intervened, quoting a Hadith of the Prophet where a case of instant triple talaq was brought before him. The Prophet asked the woman if she agreed to the talaq pronounced by her husband. When the woman answered in the negative, he asked the couple to go home and resume their marital life. Triple talaq pronounced in a single sitting was considered a single, revocable divorce by the Prophet, with the couple going back to their married life. Sattar was subjected to much ridicule and relentless criticism, and was forced to temporarily relocate to Calcutta, and then finally to Delhi after a few years.

Incidentally, both Rahman in Calcutta and Sattar in Assam were expected to use the ruling of Caliph Umar to decide the marital status of the complainants. The caliph's ruling had attained great popularity, and almost total acceptance, among the Muslims in the country, most of whom were followers of Imam Abu Hanifa, who regarded triple talaq in a single sitting as valid. It had a lot to do with the patriarchal ways of our society; women were supposed to live at the beck and call of men and in many ways stay obliged to them for the simple security of matrimony. What better weapon to wield than triple talaq, a simple action that would send their life into a tailspin? So when a couple of clerics ignored this ruling of the caliph, taking recourse to the decisions of the Prophet, a lot of furore followed. Nobody spoke a word against the ruling of the Prophet (equally importantly, nobody followed it either), but many spoke aloud that the caliph could not be wrong either.

A few years after the Calcutta and Assam incidents, there was a potentially bigger case of triple talaq in Delhi. Much like the modern-day Shayara Bano or Aafreen Rehman, back in 1980, Rukhsar was faced with the reality of instant talaq. Unlike Bano or Rehman, she, however, did not have to knock at the doors of the Supreme Court for justice. She found help next door, literally.

A resident of Gali Gaddihya near Jama Masjid, Rukhsar belonged to the lower middle class, and lived in a joint family with her husband and his parents. One evening, her husband picked a quarrel with his father. Soon, his wife intervened on his behalf. In doing so, she lost her temper and ended up using inappropriate language for her father-in-law, forcing the old man to retreat to his room. Enraged, her husband pronounced instant talaq, leaving his wife, who was by then making chapattis for the family, cowering in a corner. As he screamed his lungs out, she put both her hands on her ears to avoid listening to him. No such luck. So loud was her husband's proclamation that even the neighbours heard him. One of the women in the neighbourhood took Rukhsar to her house for the night, leaving the husband to mull over his action. The next morning, he realized his folly and wanted his wife back. He spoke to a number of clerics in the walled city. All of them expressed helplessness in restoring his conjugal rights, adding, ever so feebly, that his marriage was as good as over.

Calling the divorce talaq-e-biddat, they admonished the man, even sympathized with his dilemma, but said they couldn't consider it a single or revocable divorce. They took recourse to Imam Hanafi's ruling on the subject, where talaq followed by repeated pronouncements at the same time is considered final divorce. Incidentally, talaq-e-biddat means 'innovated (or sinful) form of divorce', something that the honourable Supreme Court struck down as a means of ending marriage in its judgment on the subject in August 2017. The Hanafis believe that though this form of divorce is innovated and sinful, it is nevertheless valid. The Hanafi stance is no different from the stance of imams Malik and Shafi'i. The Hanbalis, though, look at it differently.

Only at the insistence of the chastened husband did the clerics ponder over other options and guide him to a local alim, Mufti Abdul Dayam. He was an expert in the interpretation of the Quranic word and an authority on the Hadith. Rukhsar's case could have hit the headlines, but that was averted due to the mufti's timely intervention and sane advice. He believed talaq was the last resort for any husband and wife, not the first salvo to be fired in case of a small misunderstanding, a little spat. Following the Hanbali scholar, Ibn Taimiyah (1268–1328), the mufti, a seasoned cleric who used to teach at the historic Fatehpuri Masjid, sorted out the matter amicably. In this particular case, the husband, in a fit of rage, had pronounced talaq, talaq, talaq. The mufti scolded the man for his foul temper, but, to his relief, regarded triple talaq in one go as only a single, revocable divorce. It meant the man got a second chance at life with his wife. The two resumed cohabitation immediately and a sinful form of divorce was averted with enlightened reasoning.

A similar ruling saved the day at the height of the Babri Masjid–Ram Janmabhoomi agitation in the early 1990s. Back then, a cleric from Hyderabad was presented with a case of instant triple talaq by a resident of Rampur in Uttar Pradesh. The cleric was on a tour of the state to present the viewpoint of the Babri Masjid Action Committee when this instance of divorce was reported to him for judgment. A few days later, he had gone to Bombay to deliver another talk on the masjid issue. There, however, he consulted the Ahl-e-Hadith ulema and was happy to tell the husband that the instant triple talaq he had pronounced was revocable, and he could resume cohabitation with his wife. It saved a potentially dangerous situation from becoming the stuff of headlines in those charged times. Incidentally, the man was Hanafi, but in the spirit of eclecticism, the decision was arrived at to give his married life a second chance, much to the relief of the couple.

Incidentally, the Hanafis (most Indian Muslims are followers of Imam Abu Hanifa—some estimates go as high as 90 per cent) believe that when triple talaq is pronounced, instant divorce takes place and the wife becomes haram for her husband. He cannot take his divorce back. Nor can he remarry her with a fresh nikah. The only way she can come back to him is if she marries another man, consummates that marriage, and he divorces her. It is this interpretation that has also given rise to cases of halala, something totally against the letter and spirit of the Quran.

There are scholars like Maulana Umar Ahmad Usmani, who believe that the validation for triple talaq comes not only from Imam Abu Hanifa but also from Imam Malik and Imam Shafi'i, with only the Hanbalis being different. Incidentally, the four major schools of Sunni law—Hanafi, Maliki, Shafi'i and Hanbali—differ from one another only on the basis of their interpretation of Quranic verses and the Hadith. But they all derive their law from the same source: Quran and Hadith. However, the belief in each that only their interpretation of a particular verse or Sunna is correct leads to a difference of opinion. It gives rise to what Islamic scholars call the doctrine of *tamazzhub* and *taqleed*, wherein the adherents exalt the pronouncements of their imam/school (tamazzhub), ignoring all faculties of critical appraisal (taqleed) and accepting everything at face value. However, an eclectic choice must be opted for in case of different opinions, as advocated by Prof. Furqan Ahmed in *Triple Talaq: An Analytical Study with Emphasis on Socio-legal Aspects*.

It is claimed that after Imam Abu Hanifa's ruling, the other imams decided to follow him rather than chart their own course on the subject. However, there is no evidence to support the claim that Imam Malik and Imam Shafi'i followed Imam Abu Hanifa on the legality of instant triple talaq. Noted contemporary Islamic scholar A. Faizur Rahman is of the same opinion. He feels that historical accounts suggest that individual conclusions of all imams were based on an authentic Hadith available to them at that point of time. For example, Imam Malik's approval of the view that the triple pronouncement of talaq breaks the marriage irrevocably was based on the following Hadith, which the imam himself lists in the Kitab-al-Talaq of his collection *Muwatta*:

'Yahya related to me from Malik from Ibn Shihab that Marwan ibn al-Hakam decided that if someone made three pronouncements of divorce (*Yu tallaqu amraatahu al batta anna ha salaasa tatleegat*), he had divorced his wife irrevocably.'

Malik said, 'That is what I like best of what I have heard on the subject.' From this, Rahman concludes that it is clear that Imam Malik based his view not on Imam Abu Hanifa's interpretation, but on the judgement of Marwan ibn al-Hakam, an Umayyad caliph who laid down the law that an *al-batta* talaq counted as three divorces. Terminologically, it refers to 'the intention to permanently divorce' the wife.

However, the Hanafis are not monolithic. There is scope for dissension and debate. Some Hanafi jurists, like Hajjaj bin Artat and Muhammad ibn Muqatil, are of the opinion that if one pronounces three divorces, that is, instant triple talaq, no irrevocable divorce will take place. Similarly, there is no unity of opinion on Imam Malik either. According to Imam Tilmisani, Imam Malik also believed that only one divorce takes place if three divorces are pronounced.

Further, it is argued that Imam Ahmad bin Hanbal revised his initial opinion, deciding it was not a final divorce but a single divorce. Imam Hanbal's changed position with respect to divorce was proved by Imam Taimiyah, who said Imam Hanbal reflected on the Quranic verses about divorce and came to the conclusion that triple talaq in one go could only be considered as a single divorce or *raj'i* talaq. It meant that the husband had the right to take back his wife during the iddat period of three cycles. He could even go in for a fresh nikah if the iddat period expired. This is the position favoured by most companions of the Prophet too, among them Caliph Abu Bakr, Caliph Ali and Abdullah bin Masud.

Today, the followers of the Ahl-e-Hadith sect, said to be the most pure followers of the tradition of the Prophet, regard instant talaq as only a revocable divorce. It is their stand that is reflected in the Supreme Court judgment of 22 August 2017. The Shias too think likewise. The Ithna Asharis consider instant talaq as only a single, revocable divorce.

However, the best word against instant talaq comes from those who quote Imam Hanifa as saying that 'if you find a contradiction between my words and action with respect to the Quran, follow the book, not me'. Since nowhere does the Quran mention instant talaq, triple talaq stands invalidated. A point to be noted is that Imam Hanifa did not record his own understanding of what the Prophet said or did. His disciples, Imam Abu Yusuf and Imam Muhammad, did that immediately after his death. So there is no direct word from Imam Hanifa on triple talaq.

5

Halala: A Mischievous Interpretation

Tehseen was married in the first flush of youth. Once she passed standard VIII in West Bengal, her poor parents decided it was time to get her married. After all, by marrying Waqar, she would be shifting to Delhi. In his early twenties, Waqar was a mason and a distant relative of Tehseen on her mother's side. Tehseen's elder sister was married to Waqar's elder brother, and she seemed pretty content with her husband and the two kids he sired in a little under three years of marriage.

Tehseen, though, was not as fortunate. Barely a month into matrimony, she was divorced by her irate husband. 'Talaq, talaq, talaq,' he pronounced in the courtyard of his ancestral home in Bihar. His mother and a handful of other relatives stood as mute witnesses. Tehseen was led out of the house immediately by her mother-in-law. Back in West Bengal, her parents consulted local maulanas. There was no way forward, they ruled. The marriage was over. There were witnesses to the talaq.

Two weeks later, Tehseen's husband came to his senses. He wanted his wife back and went to her ancestral place. Tehseen's parents, who had consulted clerics, declined. However, Tehseen too wanted to go back to her husband. Nothing doing, ruled the clerics. She was haram for him, they insisted. In their minds, multiple pronouncements of the word 'talaq' at one time ended marriage as quickly as the words were completed. There was no way back, no chance to atone. Nothing. They refused to consider the Hanbali ruling, whereby multiple pronouncements at one time constituted only a revocable divorce. Tehseen and Waqar's marriage was over. Unless, of course, she did a halala!

The little girl had no idea about halala. 'It is a way to punish the man for his foul temper. What can be worse than to have your wife sleep with another man?' the imam of the local masjid in West Bengal's 24 Parganas added.

'*Lekin yeh to aurat ko saza ho gayi* (But this is a punishment for the woman),' Tehseen said, ruling out a halala arrangement.

She was among the luckier ones. Indeed, if there is one provision of marriage which is routinely made a mockery of in our society, it has to be the concept of halala. So much so that many marriages, which could have been saved had the concept of halala not been rampantly applied, have been destroyed—even Tehseen and Waqar's marriage could have been saved by simply regarding instant triple talaq as one divorce, not irrevocable. Even at the conclusion of the iddat period, they could have married each other again. Simple. There is almost complete ignorance about halala in our society.

Most maulanas have no clear view on it. And they often do grave injustice to the Quranic provision either due to their ignorance or wilful misinterpretation.

In the recent Shayara Bano case, the Attorney General of India made a forceful plea to the Supreme Court to invalidate nikah halala and polygamy alongside instant triple talaq. The court initially declined, but a few days later, as the hearing on instant triple talaq continued, the bench agreed to consider the invalidation of halala and polygamy. 'It will be dealt with in future,' the bench clarified. However, if the bench had made time to consider the halala case, or if in the future it invalidates the practice, it would be a huge relief to women who end up paying the price for either their husband's foul temper or the clerics' ignorance. Either way, men err, women suffer.

Halala, in the religious book, is a chance given to an irrevocably divorced couple to come back in matrimony, if so desired mutually. The Quran makes two divorces revocable. Within the three-month iddat period, a man can cancel the divorce through the spoken word, or by establishing physical relations. If, however, he fails to do either within the iddat period, but has a change of heart after that, he may enter into a fresh nikah. The wife is not required to marry another man first. The two can become husband and wife again with a fresh nikah and mahr. This can be done immediately at the end of the iddat period, or any time in the future as long as the woman does not marry another man.

However, in case the first divorce is revoked, but the man pronounces divorce for the second time, then the same proceedings have to be repeated. He can, once again, revoke divorce through word or intimacy. Failing to do either within the waiting period would mean that the marriage is over. Again, after the iddat period, if he wants his wife back, and she too is willing, they can have a nikah without any third-party involvement.

If, however, he pronounces divorce for the third time, she becomes a completely independent woman, totally prohibited for her erstwhile husband. At the conclusion of her iddat period, she is free to do whatever she would like to. She may choose to marry another man or stay single. In case she marries another man and he dies, or he pronounces divorce according to the procedure accepted in Islam, then she enters the iddat period again. This time, she is the widow or divorcee of the second husband. At the conclusion of the iddat period, she is once again an independent woman. Now, if she feels that instead of choosing a third partner, she would rather go back to her first husband through a new nikah, she is allowed to do so, provided the husband is willing too. Now, she is halal for him. It is this concept of a woman's independence in Islam which has been made a mockery of by ignoramuses.

The way it often pans out is, if a woman has had an irrevocable (instant triple talaq is considered irrevocable by some) divorce and expresses a desire to go back to her husband, as in Tehseen's case, a local maulana suggests halala—that is, she marries another man, obtains a divorce, completes her iddat period, and then marries her first husband again. Since it is almost impossible to find a man who would assuredly divorce the woman, often, local clerics offer their services. Under this, a nikah is conducted between the cleric and the girl, with the clear understanding of divorce the next day or a few days later. The whole exercise is hush-hush, unlike the way suggested in Islam, where a man is asked to throw a reception after the nikah so that nobody can cast aspersions on the integrity of the woman in the future. In such a twisted form of halala, everything is done under the cover of night, with barely any witnesses. It is almost like legalized prostitution. As the All India Muslim Personal Law Board (AIMPLB) submitted before the court:

> [There are] unequivocal and unambiguous Hadiths of the Prophet Muhammad (PBUH) where mock marriages and mock divorces are reported to be a cause of curse from the Almighty Allah. It is in the said Hadiths that the reference to the term Halala is found, though it is not mentioned in the Noble Quran. Whereas in any case, the term 'Nikah Halala' is not found even in [the] Hadith. The Hadiths of the Prophet Muhammad (Peace Be upon Him) in condemning Halala are as follows: 'Allah's curse is on the one who makes a contract or agreement for Halala (Both the one who carries out Halala and the one who it is done for'(Sunan al Darami/Mishkat al Masabih), and 'Allah has cursed the *muhallil* (one who marries a woman and divorces her so that she can go back to her first husband) and the *muhallal lahu* (first husband)'.

Simply put, such a wedding has no Islamic sanction. It is akin to taking a bull on hire, as is done in rural areas to enable cows to procreate. Except in this form of marriage, there is no procreation, just recreation for the man and humiliation for the woman, who ends up suffering in multiple ways because of her husband's temper.

This goes against the letter and spirit of verse 230 of Surah Baqarah, which states:

> And if a husband divorces his wife (a third time), then he cannot, after that, re-marry her until after she has married another husband and he has divorced her. In that case, there is no blame on either of them if they reunite provided they feel that they can keep the limits set forth by Allah. Such are the limits set by Allah, which He makes plain to those who understand.

This verse has to be seen against the backdrop of the atmosphere then prevalent in the Arab world. Many men were prone to divorcing their women, then taking them back, and divorcing them again. It had become a game. This process went on innumerable times. The Quran put a limit to this: a man could only divorce his wife two times. If he did so for the third time, he could not have her back, and she was free to marry any man she chose. Only a handful of legal experts have understood the halala provision in letter and spirit. It is meant to empower a woman.

Today, the way halala is used defeats the purpose of the restriction. Any nikah with a pre-agreed date and time of divorce is not allowed in Islam. It is like muta, a short-term marriage, which again is frowned upon. Marriage is a bond that can be ended only under exceptional circumstances. A woman is not a plaything to be enjoyed at night, discarded in the morning and sent back to her former husband. Yet, the way this provision is violated in our society can enrage the calmest of persons. Worse, its mischievous misinterpretation is foisted on women already reeling under the after-effects of instant triple talaq. The victims are always women, more in rural areas than urban, and the execution of the halala is starkly similar. A man pronounces divorce in a fit of rage. A little later, once his anger subsides, he realizes his folly and approaches a local cleric for a way out. The husband now wants to reconcile. She too is willing, the argument often being that he did not mean triple talaq, only a single, revocable divorce. Or that he was not in his senses when he pronounced the three dreaded words. Yet, when the maulana is consulted, he hardly ever rules that instant triple talaq given in one go without following the procedure prescribed in the Quran is only a single, revocable divorce. Instead of doing what the Prophet did when faced with such a situation—the Prophet allowed a man who had divorced his wife in this manner to go back to her if he so desired, thus giving him a chance to resume his marriage—most maulanas never ask the couple if they would like to resume their marriage. They simply consider instant triple talaq a valid, irrevocable divorce, though they refer to it as talaq-e-biddat or sinful divorce. It stands to reason: if something is sinful, how can it be allowed by a scripture? And if it is not allowed by the Quran, how can it be valid? Even the prevalent practice of halala is not supported by the Quran.

6

The Quran on Polygamy

And if you fear that you might not treat the orphans justly,
then marry the women that seem good to you: two, or three, or
four. If you fear that you will not be able to treat them justly,
then marry (only) one, or marry from among those whom your
right hands possess. This will make it more likely that you will
avoid injustice.

—Verse 3, Surah Nisa

You will not be able to treat your wives with absolute justice,
not even when you keenly desire to do so. It suffices (in order
to follow the Law of Allah that) you incline not wholly to one,
leaving the other in suspense. If you act rightly and remain God-
fearing, surely Allah is All-Forgiving, All-Compassionate.

—Verse 129, Surah Nisa

These verses from chapter four of the Quran deal with, as is obvious, polygamy. They permit a man to marry up to four women. He is instructed to be just and fair to them. Upon his inability to be so, he is advised to marry just one.

In the *Shayara Bano vs the Union of India and Others* case, the petitioners asked the Supreme Court to declare polygamy, alongside talaq-e-biddat and nikah halala, illegal and unconstitutional on the grounds that they violated the rights guaranteed by the Constitution of India under Articles 14, 15, 21 and 25.

The court limited itself to hearings on instant triple talaq, leaving nikah halala and polygamy for an unspecified future date.

Shayara Bano contended that a perusal of the decisions of the honourable court in cases like *Prakash vs Phulavati* (supra), *Javed and Others vs State of Haryana and Others*, (2003) 8 SCC 369, and *Smt. Sarla Mudgal, president, Kalyani and Others vs Union of India and Others*, (1995) 3 SCC 635 illustrated the following:

> The practice of polygamy has been recognized as injurious to public morals and it can be superseded by the state just as it can prohibit human sacrifice or the practice of Sati. In fact, in the case of Khursheed Ahmad Khan vs State of Uttar Pradesh and Others, (2015) 8 SCC 439, this Hon'ble (Supreme) Court has also taken the view that practices permitted or not prohibited by a religion do not become a religious practice or a positive tenet of the religion, since a practice does not acquire the sanction of religion merely because it is permitted. It is accordingly submitted that a ban on polygamy has long been the need of the hour in the interest of public order

and health. It is further submitted that this Hon'ble
Court has already expressed the view that polygamy is
not an integral part of religion and Article 25 merely
protects religious faith, but not practices which may run
counter to public order, morality or health.

The petitioners wanted the apex court to prohibit
polygamy as it was considered anti-women, a practice
which compromised the status of the wife and also her
fundamental rights as a citizen of India.

Further, it was argued by two of the respondents,
Zakia Soman and Noorjehan Safia Niaz, that these verses
were revealed for specific circumstances then prevailing in
the Arab world. They do not apply today, they reckoned.

'There are verses in the Quran which allow
marriage up to four times (4:3). This particular verse is
a contextual verse which was revealed after the Battle
of Uhud, when a large number of men were killed and
many women were rendered widows and orphaned.
It was to provide protection of their property and to
prevent injustice happening to them that this particular
verse was revealed. It has a particular specific context,'
says Noorjehan, arguing that another verse in the same
surah has a normative application. 'The verse (4:129) is
a normative verse which is for all times to come. The
Quran has many verses which are contextual, which
were revealed to tackle a particular situation existing
then. But there are also verses which point to moving
towards a better and just society. It says even if it is your
ardent desire to treat your multiple wives equally, you

cannot, so marry one. Sadly, all contextual verses are quoted, but the Quran's vision of moving towards better society is quietly ignored.'

When the petitioners sought a ban on nikah halala, they stood on solid ground with respect to the Quran, for the book nowhere mentions halala the way it is often carried out in our country. However, when it comes to the verses on polygamy, they are not on as strong a footing as is there is scope for interpreting the specific aims and objectives of the verses concerned.

Setting aside the specific or immediate-versus-timeless debate on the said verses, a simple look at the history of nikah and talaq in the country would clear the picture. Without needing any prohibition from the state or the courts, such a condition can be inserted into the nikahnama when the marriage is being solemnized. In fact, this has been done for centuries. Right from the days of the Delhi Sultanate and the Mughals, polygamy or bigamy has been all but prohibited. There is evidence that conditions preventing a man from taking another wife were incorporated into various nikahnamas. If, after the nikah, the man flouted this condition, the marriage stood dissolved. In some cases, the man was allowed to take another wife, but certain conditions applied. These included the permission of the first wife. Often, the second wife would live separately and not come to the dwelling of the first wife on any occasion without her prior approval.

In his book *Divorce and Gender Equity in Muslim Personal Law of India*, Dr Kauser Edappagath, then a district and sessions judge in Kerala, noted the well-known *Sainuddin vs Latifannessa Bibi* case, where the husband had vested his power of divorce with his wife in the nikahnama. In the nikahnama, Sainuddin agreed not to marry a second wife without the consent of the first wife, not to beat or ill-treat the wife and to allow her to visit her parents. When the husband did marry for the second time, his wife left him. The husband filed a case for restitution of his conjugal rights, whereupon she divorced herself three times in accordance with Muslim law under the authority vested in her at the time of the nikah. The court accepted her plea that she was no longer his wife, so there was no case for restitution of conjugal rights.

Similarly, in the *Badrunnissa vs Mafiatalla* case, the Calcutta High Court held:

> Where a husband had entered into a private agreement with his wife authorizing her to divorce him upon his marrying a second wife during her life, and without her consent, the wife on proof of her husband married a second time without her consent was entitled to divorce.

Incidentally, talaq-e-tafweez is prevalent and respected across the country. It is fully applicable, as stated by Dr Edappagath. The Muslim Personal Law (Shariat) Application Act, 1937, specifically mentions this form of divorce. If monogamy can be a clause for a nikah to be solemnized, the debate on the details or applicability of the verses gets silenced. However, among Islamic scholars, there is little support for Noorjehan and Zakia

Soman's arguments. In Tafsir ibn Kathir, it is stated that Allah restricted the number of wives to four as at that time, many men were prone to keeping multiple wives, occasionally hundreds. As Tafsir ibn Kathir reveals:

> Yet, men are prohibited from marrying more than four wives, as the Ayah decrees, since the Ayah specifies that men are allowed four wives, as Ibn Abbas and the majority of scholars stated . . . Imam Ahmad recorded that Salim said that his father said that Ghilan bin Salamah Ath-Thafaqi had ten wives when he became Muslim, and the Prophet said to him, 'Choose any four of them (and divorce the rest).' During the reign of Umar, Ghilan divorced his remaining wives [as well] and divided his money between his [three] children. When Umar heard of this, he said to Ghilan, 'I think that the devil has conveyed to your heart the news of your imminent death, from what the devil hears during his eavesdropping . . . By Allah! You will take back your wives and your money, or I will take possession of this all.

Therefore, if men were allowed to have more than one wife—up to four—only in specific circumstances caused due to the loss of life and property, as in the Battle of Uhud, the Prophet and the caliph would have asked Ghilan to limit himself to one wife. The fact that the Prophet asked him to keep four proves that a man is allowed to marry four women in normal circumstances. The Prophet's ruling was supported by the decision of the caliph, who scolded Ghilan and warned him of dire consequences for his decision to divorce the remaining three women. Had the caliph too thought that a man was allowed to marry only one woman, he would have hailed Ghilan for divorcing three women!

Further, as stated by Sayyid Abul Ala Mawdudi (translated by Zafar Ishaq Ansari) in *Towards Understanding the Quran*, there are other instances from Islamic history to buttress the contention that the said verses of Surah Nisa are for all times to come. With respect to verse 3, he gives three views, one of them by the Prophet's wife, Aisha. She is reported to have said:

> . . . men tended to marry orphan girls who were under their guardianship out of consideration for either their property, beauty or because they thought they would be able to treat them according to their whims, as they had no one to protect them. After marriage, such men sometimes committed excesses against these girls. It is in this context that the Muslims are told that if they fear they will not be able to do justice to the orphan girls, then they should marry other girls whom they like.

This interpretation is supported by verse 127 of the same surah.

The viewpoint of revered scholar Ibn Abbas and his disciple Ikrimah is more forthright. As reproduced by Mawdudi, they expressed the following opinion:

> In the Jahiliyah (ignorance) period there was no limit on the number of wives a man could take. The result

was that a man sometimes married as many as ten women, and, when expenses increased because of a large family, he encroached on the rights either of his orphan nephews or other relatives. It was in this context that God fixed the limit of four wives and instructed the Muslims that they marry up to four wives providing they possessed the capacity to treat them equitably.

The surah upholds the right of a woman to honourable and just treatment at the hands of her husband. As stated by Mawdudi:

> Muslim jurists agreed that according to this verse the maximum number of wives has been fixed at four. This conclusion is also supported by Islamic traditions. It is reported that when Ghilan, the chief of Taif, embraced Islam, he had nine wives (according to another commentary, it is ten). The Prophet (peace be upon him) ordered him to keep only four wives and divorce the rest. Another person, Nawfal B. Mu'awiyah, had five wives. The Prophet (peace be on him) ordered him to divorce one of them. This verse stipulates that marrying more wives is permissible on the condition that one treats his wives equitably. A person who avails himself of this permission granted by God to have a plurality of wives, and disregards the condition laid down by God to treat them equitably, has not acted in good faith with God.

Also, there is a Hadith about maintaining multiple wives. The Prophet is reported to have stated: 'If one has two wives and does not treat them justly, he will appear on the Day of Judgement as one afflicted with paralysis.'

Yes, the Quran did not aim to put an end to polygamy. It placed restrictions on its free, unhindered, unchallenged practice. A man was allowed to marry four women, but upon his inability to treat them all equally, he was advised to restrict himself to just one. It neither made polygamy mandatory nor prohibited it. A woman who does not wish to share her husband is free to incorporate the clause at the time of her nikah. The same goes for the man— he can agree to such a precondition or turn it down. If he feels he cannot treat them all equally, he is better off giving all his love, attention and time to one. That would be better for him.

7

Khula: A Woman's Right to Divorce

In a world of convenient stereotypes, the Muslim woman is seen as a helpless, whimpering human being with the threat of triple talaq hanging over her head despite years of matrimony. Almost all men and women with access to newspapers would have heard of triple talaq. Not many, though, would have heard of khula, the woman's inalienable right to divorce. Worse, even Muslim women seem unaware of this right. Things get positively disappointing when one realizes that even among those who are aware of khula, there is no clarity on its provisions. There is a lack of unanimity on whether it is solely a woman's right, or, as some advocates of male supremacy contend, it is a mutual right to part ways.

Under khula, a woman has a right similar to that of a man to dissolve the marriage. What's more, she has to specify no grounds for effecting the divorce. She has to furnish no proof of harassment or ill treatment. Something as simple as a dislike for her husband's looks can be reason enough for khula to take place, as proven in Islamic history. In a well-known Hadith, it is narrated that a woman came to the Prophet and declared her intention to divorce her husband. The Prophet asked her to reconsider her decision. Thereupon, she asked the Prophet whether it was his recommendation or instruction. The Prophet said it was only a recommendation. The woman then rejected the recommendation and was granted khula.

There is a well-known incident, from the Prophet's time, about a woman called Jameela, the wife of Sabit bin Quais. She hated her husband because of how he looked. He was, however, pretty fond of her. 'If I had no fear of God, I should have struck him on the face whenever he approached me,' the woman told the Prophet. Thereupon, the Prophet asked the husband to take back the garden he was offered and divorce Jameela. This illustration shows the Prophet's recognition of the right of a Muslim wife to ask for divorce when it was clear that the parties could not live within the limits of God. It speaks volumes about the freedom a woman enjoyed during the Prophet's time. Indeed, khula has been in existence for as long as the Quran has—probably the first known instance in history where a woman has been granted the right to dissolve her marriage.

No qazi can overrule the decision of the woman. Nor can he inquire into the reasons for her action. He cannot even ask her to rethink her decision. She needs no cleric, no intermediary for this divorce to take place. All that the qazi has to do is to play the role of a facilitator and make sure that the parting does not get ugly. Under khula, a woman has to announce her intention to obtain a divorce, and the husband has to agree. In case he does not agree, the matter can be presented before the qazi, who cannot invalidate the woman's decision. He only has to make sure that she is serious about it. He then asks the man to release the woman from wedlock. No grounds have to be stated. The man cannot say no. It is a simple, irrevocable, instant divorce. The whole process, including the qazi's involvement, does not take more than a month, which is much faster than our Lok Adalats.

Unlike when talaq is pronounced by a man, a woman does not stay with her husband after khula comes into effect. There is no cooling-off period, no time to rethink the decision. And there is absolutely no need for the wife to stay on with her husband after khula. This is done to safeguard her chastity, as after khula her erstwhile husband is considered a stranger to her. If she were to stay with him, the man, being physically more powerful, could overpower her, resulting in greater ugliness and pain for both the parties.

If the man has not paid his wife the mahr before she decides to go in for khula, she cannot demand it. Some jurists feel that even if he has paid the mahr, she should surrender it. However, others point out that the Quran asks men to be generous and not take back any gifts they might have given to their spouse in happier times. The Quran, through a part of verse 229, Surah Baqarah, clears the picture. It says:

> It is not lawful for you (men) to take back any of your gifts (from your wives). Except when both parties fear

that they would be unable to keep the limits set forth
by Allah. If you (judges) do fear that they would be
unable to keep the limits set forth by Allah, then there
is no blame on either of them if she gives something
for her freedom.

As reputed Islamic scholar Maulana Muhammed Ali puts
it, 'These words give the wife the right to claim divorce.
It is one of the distinguishing characteristics of Islam, that
it gives the wife the right to claim divorce if she is willing
to forgo the whole or part of her dower.'

A khula may take place orally or through a written
document called khulnama. Like talaq, it must be seen
as the last resort, something to be used when the woman
feels she may not be able to observe the limits set by the
scripture.

Illustrious Islamic scholar Maulana Mawdudi wrote
in *Huquq al-Zawjain*:

Islamic law effects a beautiful equilibrium between
the divorce rights of men and women. It is a great
folly that we have practically withdrawn from our
women the right of Khula, little caring for the fact that
denying them the right which Shariat gives them on
a footing equal to talaq is absolutely un-Islamic. It is
indeed a mockery of the Shariat that we regard Khula
as something depending either on the consent of the
husband or on the verdict of the qazi. The law of Islam
is not responsible for the way Muslim women are
being deprived of their right in this respect.

Yet, khula is much ignored in our sociopolitical media circles. Rather than casting light on khula as one of the little-known facets of the sharia that could help women, the media generally paints Muslim women as weaklings who are denied their rights by both religion and society, and the truth seldom comes to the fore. Not that half-educated maulanas are of any help. They seldom tell their students the meaning of the Quran's verses and are often ignorant themselves. Women are rarely told about the powers vested in them by Islam. Hence, in the courts of most qazis, there are many more complaints of a man fighting to get his instant triple talaq annulled than of wives who have taken khula and are awaiting formal papers from the qazi. There have, however, been many cases of women approaching the courts of law for their right to be released from wedlock, while men have often filed complaints to get their conjugal rights back!

Khula is a form of divorce recognized by Indian law. The Muslim Personal Law (Shariat) Application Act, 1937, mentions it as a form of divorce initiated by the wife. In his book, Dr Edappagath, points out, 'The state laws for registration of Muslim marriages and divorce in force in Assam, Bihar, Meghalaya, Odissa and West Bengal also provide for registration of khula.'

However, Indian courts often tend to depend on the husband's agreement to divorce for khula to come through. As pointed out by Edappagath:

[The] Allahabad High Court also took the same view and held that: 'That a suit by a Muslim wife to compel her husband to give her khula is the sole act of the husband and to exercise such power is wholly a matter within his own discretion, and it is not demandable by the wife as a matter of right under the Muslim law.'

This is an interpretation of an Islamic provision that goes against the interests of women, as also the tradition of the Prophet. It seeks to fiddle with an established right of women.

Simply put, khula is a woman's inalienable right to divorce. Once the husband agrees, it has the effect of a single, irrevocable divorce. And the husband cannot refuse consent.

8

Other Ways for Her . . .

The invalidation of triple talaq by the honourable Supreme Court in August 2017 was received with warmth and a public expression of joy. Prime Minister Narendra Modi hailed the 3–2 verdict of the Supreme Court as 'historic', a judgment that 'grants equality to Muslim women and is a powerful weapon for women empowerment'. Considering he had spoken along almost the same lines across public fora in the months preceding Chief Justice J.S. Khehar's judgment, it was scarcely a surprise that he saw in it a tool for Muslim women's empowerment, something that would give them great marital security. Indeed, even at an election rally in Mahoba in Uttar Pradesh, he raised the subject. His sentiments were aptly expressed by his party's president Amit Shah, who reiterated: 'The judgment marks the beginning of a new era of pride and equality for Muslim women.'

Just as there is actually no mention of instant talaq in the Quran, in other aspects as well, the holy book and the Hadith of the Prophet safeguard the women. They are not as dependent on men to get out of a troublesome marriage as is widely believed. Besides the relatively better known khula, women have other ways to step out of a marriage that is not working out. Their right to dissolve a marriage is well protected by the Muslim Personal Law (Shariat) Application Act, 1937, and the Dissolution of Muslim Marriage Act, 1938. They, in addition, enjoy at least five other ways of getting rid of incompatible, violent or slanderous husbands. The conditions for this cover everything from dowry demands to casting aspersions on the character of the wife, or simply the inability to fulfil marital obligations.

The most widely practised among these other methods is talaq-e-tafweez, under which the husband vests in his wife the right to divorce him. This condition should ideally be written down at the time of marriage in the nikahnama and can go a long way in bringing down the rate of divorce. Unfortunately, hardly any nikahnama is framed in such a manner as to include this condition of divorce. Importantly, if there is space for talaq-e-tafweez in the nikahnama, it can also prevent the husband from taking another wife, thereby limiting the chances of polygamy. The wife, at the time of signing the nikahnama, can stipulate the condition that the husband will not take another wife, or at least not bring another wife to her home. The clause will safeguard her independence, and she will not have to share her home with another woman. This was a precondition in many marriages during the times of the Mughals too. In the twentieth century, both in pre- and post-Independence India, there have been a number of judicial cases involving talaq-e-tafweez.

In the well-known *Saifuddin Sekh vs Soneka Bibi* case, the Assam High Court held that an antenuptial contract be embodied in the *kabinnama* stating that in case the husband brings any of his other wives to stay with the petitioner without her consent, she would be at liberty to exercise the right to divorce. The ruling was in consonance with that of the Calcutta High Court earlier, which upheld, in the *Moharam Ali vs Ayesha Khatun* case, this kind of agreement under which the wife was authorized to divorce her husband in case he married any other woman.

Also available to Muslim women is divorce through mutual consent. It is called mubaraat. This is considered irrevocable by Sunnis as well as Shias. This out-of-court divorce finds mention in the Muslim Personal Law (Shariat) Application Act, 1937. It is very similar to what the modern-day courts often advise a quarrelling couple: settle things out of court in the presence of an advocate. The only difference in divorce by mubaraat is that there is no need for an advocate.

Women facing infringement of their personal space or confronted with a philandering husband can also apply for *faskh*, or judicial divorce. Here, she has to move an application before a qazi, who can annul the marriage on her application. Of course, there have to be valid grounds for something as serious as faskh to take place— for instance, when the whereabouts of the husband are not known for four years, as was the case in Kashmir at

the height of insurgency when many men were reported
missing for years, leaving their wives in a state of half-
widowhood. In such cases, the woman can annul the
marriage and move on with her life. Similarly, faskh can be
resorted to if the husband fails to provide maintenance for
two years or is unable to discharge his conjugal obligations.
In other words, impotency provides a woman grounds for
divorce. Similarly, if the husband goes insane or suffers
from a venereal disease, the wife can seek dissolution of
marriage through faskh. Importantly, as it was practised
in medieval times, the husband is not allowed to be cruel
to his wife. Besides marital violence, cruelty includes
taking in another woman. If a clause against bigamy is
inserted into the nikahnama, it helps a woman dissolve
the marriage either through talaq-e-tafweez or faskh.

Also, Islamic law protects the integrity of marriage
and the reputation of the woman. The Quran through
Surah Nur, verse 4, states, 'Those who accuse chaste,
honourable women (of unchastity) but do not produce
four witnesses, flog them with eighty lashes, and do
not admit their testimony ever after. They are indeed
transgressors.' And for husbands who do accuse their
wives of immoral conduct, verse 6 says:

> As for those who accuse their wives (of unchastity), and
> have no witnesses except themselves: the testimony
> of such a one is that he testify, swearing by Allah four
> times, that he is truthful (in his accusation), and a fifth
> time, that the curse of Allah be on him if he is lying (in
> his accusation). And the punishment shall be averted

from the woman if she were to testify, swearing by Allah four times that the man was lying, and a fifth time that the wrath of Allah be on her if the man be truthful (in his accusation).

If the husband charges his wife with adultery, and is not able to back it up with evidence, she is entitled to obtain a divorce called lian. This is a distinct form of divorce that is recognized by the Shariat Act, 1937.

Back in 1977, in the *Noorjahan Bibi vs Mohammed Kazim Ali* case, the latter was found guilty of making a false accusation against Bibi. Upon his inability to substantiate his charges, the court dissolved Bibi's marriage under the provision of lian. Again, this is not an option exercised often by Indian women, as one can make out from the story of Atiya Sabri, who was falsely charged by her husband, yet stayed on in matrimony, giving him a chance to end the marriage through instant triple talaq. Had she sought dissolution of marriage under lian, she would have been well within her rights. The situation can be blamed on the conditioning, or simple ignorance, of Muslim society.

Islam also offers a remedy to those trapped in a child marriage. If a girl is given away in marriage in the age of innocence, she can cancel it when she becomes an adult. This kind of divorce can be effected after the onset of puberty and is called *khyar-ul-bulugh*.

9

Divorce Methods of the Shias

The glorious Quran is universal and eternal. It belongs to the entire humanity, as much to a Muslim as a non-Muslim, as applicable to a Sunni as a Shia. The chapters and verses dealing with divorce are the same for both sects. Verses from Surah Baqarah, Surah Nisa and Surah Talaq are quoted both by Shias and Sunnis when it comes to deciding cases of talaq. Why then is talaq much more difficult, and less practised, among the Shias than the Sunnis? Well, the answer lies in the Quran, in adhering to its message before all else.

While a section of the Sunnis lays great stock by Caliph Umar's administrative action, there are no such problems with the Shias. For this community, the word of the Quran is followed, practised and upheld before everything else, including some Hadith whose authenticity may not be vouched for by all.

The first step in trying to avoid a divorce is mutual consultation between the husband and wife. The spouses are advised to talk to each other and sort out their issues in a spirit of generosity and forgiveness. They are even encouraged to give each other space to overcome any perceived problems. This could be as simple as the spouses not sleeping in the same bed or in the same room. It could include staying away from each other for a few days. This advice to a couple is equally respected by both the Sunnis and the Shias. It is, however, at the next stage that the first difference between the communities crops up.

Among the Sunnis, if the spouses fail to arrive at a solution, two arbiters, one from each side, are appointed. Among the Shias, the number is doubled, with two witnesses from each side. This casts the net of possible reconciliation a bit wider. The involvement of more people means more talking heads and more opportunity to thrash out the issue in the privacy of the home rather than going through a public divorce. Further, there is often the involvement of the community elders and the clergymen. The imams use their considerable influence on the community to prevail upon the warring spouses to overlook each other's drawbacks and resume cohabitation. This strong social support system is not always as visible among the Sunnis, where instant triple talaq can be a self-destructive weapon for ignorant spouses.

Both Sunnis and Shias agree on talaq-e-ahsan and talaq-e-hasan, that is, single pronouncement of divorce followed by a three-month iddat period, and monthly pronouncement of divorce for three months, respectively. In the Shia community, however, there is no concept of instant triple talaq, which Sunni Hanafis often follow.

Divorce always has to be spaced out, with at least a month's gap between each pronouncement. Upon the failure of the local imam, the community and family elders to effect reconciliation, the couple is allowed to part ways. But for any divorce to take place, the physical presence of the spouses is a must. No husband can divorce his wife in her absence. Equally necessary is the presence of two witnesses. This rules out instant triple talaq through text messages, WhatsApp messages, emails, speed post or even the telephone or Skype. The written word is not good enough. There has to be an oral pronouncement of talaq by the man. For the Shias, talaq can only be expressed or delegated—talaq-e-tafweez. For the Sunnis, however, it can be expressed, delegated or even implied. Among the Shias, too, a talaq pronounced under the influence of liquor (forced or voluntary consumption) or coercion is invalid. Besides, any ambiguity on the part of the husband in the pronouncement of divorce renders it void. There is a section of Hanafi Sunnis that believes a pronouncement of divorce in jest also holds good for a valid divorce. But the Shias believe that a pronouncement of divorce in jest is not valid under the Fiqh Jafari school of jurisprudence. Further—and here is a similarity with the Sunnis—only one pronouncement can be made in one month or one menstrual cycle. It is important to note that any incidence of sexual intimacy between the couple during a cycle renders null and void a pronouncement of divorce made during that cycle. For any pronouncement of divorce, the man and the woman must not have had physical relations during the said period.

Three successive pronouncements in three separate months lead to a final, irrevocable divorce. There is a similarity with the Sunnis here: the man can revoke divorce through the spoken word or physical action during the period and the divorce(s) pronounced stand(s) cancelled.

There is, however, a difference between the two sects when it comes to the concept of ila, or constructive divorce. Among the Sunnis, a husband may take an oath to not establish physical relations with his wife. If he deliberately does not have physical relations with her for four months, the marriage is irrevocably dissolved. However, under the Shias' Ithna Ashra school, ila becomes valid only after an order of a court of law. At the conclusion of four months, the wife may apply for a judicial divorce, or she may file a plea for restitution of conjugal rights. In other words, ila is not an unchallenged right of the husband among the Shias.

Similarly, on the question of zihar—that is, divorce through an unnatural comparison by the husband—the Shias require the presence of two witnesses at the time of the utterance. Here, however, as with the Sunnis, the husband has a four-month period to render the divorce null by simply resuming cohabitation with his wife. If he would like to do so at the conclusion of the fourth month, he still has that option. However, it comes with a condition: he would have to fast for two months, or provide food to at least sixty people, or free a slave.

In the mubaraat system of divorce, too, there is a difference between the sects. Among the Sunnis, if both the husband and wife want to move on, there are no impediments in their path. Among the Shias, however, there has to be a valid reason, accompanied by a proper form. The parties concerned must specify it all in Arabic, if they know the language. Once effective, however, mubaraat is an irrevocable divorce for both sects. No intervention by the courts is required. If, during the iddat period of mubaraat, a woman goes back on her promise of paying an agreed sum, the man can also reconcile, and they remain husband and wife without a fresh nikah. The money received by the man from the woman at the time of talaq mubaraat should be less than the mahr. But under khula it can be more than the mahr.

However, when it comes to matters of divorce, it is not only in the social support system and the oral pronouncement of the word that the Shias differ from the Sunnis. They differ at the first stage too, the nikah. Among members of the community, any nikah is supposed to be accompanied by two things: *aqd* and mahr, the former being the proposal and the terms and conditions of the marriage mooted by the first party and agreed upon by the other, the latter loosely being the dower or a woman's due. While this condition is not always met by all Shia nikahs, the Sunni nikahnamas hardly ever have any precondition. There is only the mention of mahr, besides the names and addresses, temporary and permanent, of the spouses, along with the names and signatures of the advocate and witnesses. Among the Shias, an effort is made at negotiation between the two parties. It helps to prevent any misunderstanding later, and probably goes some way in bringing down the divorce rate in the community.

Pertinently, at the time of a Shia girl's first marriage, her father's assent is regarded as enough for the nikah to take place. Obviously, it is seconded by the girl, but either the father or the paternal grandfather has to give his nod as well. In another departure from Sunni traditions, the girl is given in nikah by a family elder or witness. There is no concept of the client–procurer relationship among the Sunnis; the girl is not given away in marriage by her father or a male elder.

Also, it is not necessary to have two witnesses at the time of nikah for any Shia marriage to be solemnized. Witnesses are required at the time of divorce, not during the nikah. Even a woman can become an attorney and say the *seegha-e-nikah* (the formula for nikah). It is not necessary that only a man say the seegha-e-nikah. The man and woman can also appoint just one attorney to say the seegha-e-nikah for them. They even have the option of saying it themselves to solemnize a marriage.

There is also an important difference in the matter of mahr. Though now it is practised more among people with lower income levels, the mahr in the Shia community is often mahr-e-Fatimi, that is, the mahr Hazrat Fatima, the daughter of the Prophet, got at the time of her wedding. Her husband, who would later become Caliph Ali, was not a rich man. All he could offer was a saddle, which he sold for some money to procure the bare minimum household items. To this day, many Shias keep the amount of mahr equivalent to the money the saddle would have procured in the open market today. Others, though, have moved with the times. They fix the mahr according to the earning capacity of the groom. Thus, the mahr amount for a man earning handsomely is likely to be much more than the mahr-e-Fatimi.

Also, it is said that a section of Shias believes in muta, or short-term marriage for a pre-fixed period, though it is seldom practised in the subcontinent and very rarely in India. At the conclusion of the agreed period, the man and woman automatically stand divorced unless they want to continue. This provision of a short-term marriage is not acceptable among Sunnis, and is in fact frowned upon.

Some Sunni scholars, in their criticism of the practice of halala, call a woman's second marriage a muta or temporary marriage with a pre-decided date and time of divorce. That is not the case with Shias.

10

Divorce during the Mughal Age

During the hearing of the *Shayara Bano vs the Union of India and Others* case, women's rights activist Zakia Soman of the BMMA, through senior advocate Anand Grover, submitted that talaq-e-biddat gained validity based on acceptance by British courts. What was said was obvious, what was implied was that talaq-e-biddat had no sanctity during the times of the Mughals. 'The judgments delivered by the British courts were formally crystallized in the authoritative pronouncement by the Privy Council in the Rashid Ahmad case. Since then talaq-e-biddat has been practised,' it was submitted before the Supreme Court.

It was an interesting observation considering, before the British, the Mughals ruled over the vast expanse from Kashmir to the Deccan. The Mughals were Hanafis. Logic dictates that instant triple talaq must have been the norm under their rule. Though there are no authoritative accounts, certain farmans of the emperors, and some administrative records, prove otherwise. The Mughals had quite an evolved way of marriage wherein, at least among the upper class, the nikahnama terms and conditions were specified. Pretty often, bigamy was ruled out—interestingly, in the Supreme Court case, the petitioners wanted the court to ban nikah halala and polygamy as well. Also, marital violence was ruled out. In case either occurred, the marriage was rendered null and void. But over and above these rules was the dictate of the emperor. If he so willed, no marriage was allowed to either break or subsist. He could even overrule the qazi.

Having said that, marriage and divorce operated at the class level. The lower class, the poor, did not always have a valid nikahnama or a marriage document. Here, the word of the groom in the presence of family elders was sufficient. However, even among the poor an attempt was made to provide social and economic security to the women. The man was instructed to give his wife certain maintenance and not marry another woman. There is an instance of a man called Ibrahim who appeared as a guarantor for one Muhammad Jiu. It was agreed upon that if Jiu did not provide his wife, Maryam, one copper coin a day for sustenance and a couple of saris every year, Ibrahim would provide the same. This was in 1612. However, seven years later, in March 1619, the husband complained to the qazi saying his wife had left the house. When the wife produced the document wherein Jiu had pledged to give her maintenance of a coin a day and two saris every year, the marriage stood dissolved as Jiu and Ibrahim had failed to meet the condition for four years.

Among the more privileged ones, there was a nikahnama with the terms and conditions clearly mentioned. There are known instances when a woman held her husband to account for these conditions, and even obtained khula on his failure to fulfil them.

According to historians, four rules were laid down at the time of marriage. The first condition pertained to monogamy; the husband was instructed not to take another wife. Then, in a ruling remarkable for the seventeenth century, an attempt was made to safeguard women from domestic violence. Men were told at the time of signing the nikahnama not to indulge in marital violence. This condition was often written down in the contract. They were also told not to indulge in acts of violence towards their wives. There was also a safeguard against concubines and extramarital flings, put in place through a written condition stating that a man would not abstain from his wife for a long period. In case he had to be away for reasons of professional exigency or any other personal responsibility, he had to provide maintenance for his wife during the period. Also, as many men were often part of the army and could lay hands on slave girls with ease, conditions were incorporated into the nikahnama prohibiting the taking-in of a slave girl by a man. Or, if he did, the wife was within her right to give away that girl or to sell her and keep the money. The failure of the husband to keep his word with respect to monogamy, marital non-violence and maintenance often dissolved marriages. The nikahnama was like a modern-day marriage contract which lists conditions for settlement between spouses, as also the reasons for a possible split. Pertinently, there are no records of any qazi insisting on nikah halala or anything similar for a couple that might want to cohabit after instant triple talaq.

Though not recorded, there were cases of instant triple talaq at that time too. But it was not a rampant social phenomenon. Accepted by some qazis during the age of Akbar and Jahangir, it was denounced clearly by noted historian and theologian Abdul Qadir Badauni. He wrote in 1595 during the reign of Akbar:

> Since divorce is not only the most disapproved one among the permitted practices, resort to it is against humanity. What good tradition do the (Muslim) people have in India that they abhor the practice and regard it as the worst of evils. Indeed, some people, if any one calls them 'divorcee' would be ready to kill the abuser.

His words convey a total lack of judicial or religious acceptance of talaq-e-biddat during the Mughal Age.

Further, Badauni's words got support from Jahangir in 1611. Jahangir was known for his system of justice. In *Majalis-e-Jahangiri*, there is a record of the emperor rendering instant triple talaq inapplicable in certain conditions. It said in the record that on 20 June 1611, he ruled that a divorce pronounced by a husband in the absence of the wife was null and void. The qazi, too, agreed with the emperor. Something contradictory happened in the twentieth century when women like Atiya Sabri and Aafreen Rehman were divorced without their knowledge, and the local clerics considered the talaq valid.

Similarly, the Mughals proved to be quite visionary in protecting the rights of women in other aspects of Islamic theology. A document from Surat, dated 1628—when Shah Jahan had just taken over from his father Jahangir—records the case of a husband accepting a compensation from his wife for consenting to khula proclaimed by her. He is said to have received Rs 42 for agreeing to the dissolution of the marriage. In another instance of khula, a man was brought before a local qazi by his wife in Surat. He was told to abstain from liquor and toddy in future. Any failure on his part would mean his wife could secure divorce before the qazi. And his consent would be mandatory. He could neither delay nor deny consent. This was during Jahangir's time. His father Jalaluddin Akbar was a greater visionary. Back in the mid-sixteenth century, he sought to fix the minimum age of marriage for girls. He did not want girls to be given away in marriage before the age of puberty. The age of marriage for girls was fixed at twelve years. This rule was applicable to Hindus too.

As the Mughals, and probably the Sultans before them, were all Hanafis, Hanafism dominated India before the arrival of the British. A. Faizur Rahman, secretary general of the Chennai-based Islamic Forum for the Promotion of Moderate Thought, calls it the 'official religion' of the Muslim majority right from the time of the founding of the Mamluk dynasty in 1206, thanks to the Hanafi ulema who came with the conquerors from Central Asia. These ulema, even while relying on the rulings of medieval Hanafi legal treatises, such as the Hidaya of al-Marghinani (1196), produced their own collection of rulings to address the needs of their times. The most famous of them all was the Fatwa-e-Alamgiri. It is not just a collection of the emperor's fatwas, but a comprehensive legal text of the Hanafi law.

Considering Hanafism held sway in the country, Badauni's words and the instances reported in *Majalis-e-Jahangiri* prove that the Mughals were not averse to following the orders of other imams if the situation so demanded.

11

The Supreme Court's *Shayara Bano vs the Union of India and Others* Judgment

The Supreme Court's Constitution bench, comprising the then chief justice of India J.S. Khehar and justices Kurian Joseph, R.F. Nariman, U.U. Lalit and S. Abdul Nazeer, through a split 3–2 verdict, set aside the practice of instant triple talaq. The Constitution bench, with judges belonging to five different religions, including just one representative of the majority religion, was hearing five writ petitions filed by Muslim women who were victims of instant triple talaq. The petitions of Aafreen Rehman, Gulshan Parveen, Ishrat Jahan and Atiya Sabri were clubbed with the lead petition of Shayara Bano, who sought a direction declaring the practice of triple talaq (talaq-e-biddat), nikah halala and polygamy under the Muslim Personal Law illegal, unconstitutional and violative of the fundamental rights guaranteed to a woman under Articles 14, 15, 21 and 25 of the Constitution.

The judgment was hailed for underlining the absolute nature of freedom of religion guaranteed under the

Constitution. Many women activists called it a significant step towards gender justice. Others regarded it as the victory of Muslim women over conservative elements in the society, symbolized by the ulema. Yet, this landmark judgment almost did not come about. That it did was thanks mainly to another, totally unrelated, judgment concerning the inheritance rights of a Hindu woman.

The Supreme Court's 395-page verdict on triple talaq stemmed, incredibly, from a case of denial of rights to Hindu women under a 2005 amendment to the Hindu Succession Act. A Hindu woman had won a case in the Bombay High Court against her brothers for retrospective application of the Hindu Succession (Amendment) Act, 2005, in the *Prakash and Others vs Phulavati and Others* case. The Supreme Court, however, overruled the High Court's verdict in October 2015, holding that for the application of the Act both father and daughter had to be alive at the time of the amendment. It was then that the Bench of justices Adarsh Kumar Goel and Anil R. Dave felt that Muslim law was discriminatory too, and mooted the filing of a PIL. This came to be known as the Suo Moto Civil Writ Petition 2 of 2015. It was titled 'Muslim Women's Quest for Equality vs Jamiat Ulema-e-Hind'. It was after this that Shayara Bano filed a case to get triple talaq, halala and polygamy declared illegal. The five-judge bench struck different notes: it wasn't surprising that once the Chief Justice read out the first few lines of his judgment, wherein he called triple talaq a 1400-year-old practice, many news channels and websites ran tickers claiming, 'Supreme Court upholds triple talaq, gives govt six months to legislate'.

The Chief Justice, in his 272-page verdict, upheld the freedom of religion, stating that to uphold the petition to declare triple talaq unconstitutional would negate the freedom of religion. Refusing to strike down triple talaq, he did not find it violative of public health, order or morality—or even constitutional morality, as was sought. Nor was the practice considered contrary to the other fundamental rights enshrined in the Constitution.

The honourable Chief Justice stated: 'Talaq-e-biddat is a matter of "personal law" of Sunni Muslims . . . We have examined whether the practice satisfies the constraints provided under Article 25 (freedom to practise and propagate religion), and have arrived at the conclusion that it does not breach any of them'.

Under Article 142, he ordered that no triple talaq could take place for six months. During this time, he urged the Parliament to frame laws of reform, based on the pattern of those adopted by various Muslim countries. His judgment was agreed to by Justice Abdul Nazeer, making it a two-judge verdict.

Opposed to their judgment was that of justices Nariman and Lalit. They ruled against instant triple talaq and found that in the absence of a process of reconciliation, the act was violative of the right to equality. They based their judgment on the recognition of instant triple talaq by the Shariah Act, 1937, and found the Act violative of the Constitution to the extent that it recognized triple talaq. The honourable justices wrote:

This form of talaq must, therefore, be held to be violative of the fundamental right contained under

Article 14 of the Constitution of India. In our opinion, therefore the 1937 Act, insofar as it seeks to recognize and enforce triple talaq, is within the meaning of the expression 'laws in force' in Article 13 (1) and must be struck down as being void to the extent that it recognizes and enforces triple talaq.

The two judges also felt that triple talaq, considered sinful by the community itself, could not be protected under the freedom of religion guaranteed under Article 25. It was certainly not essential to the faith. Incidentally, it was an argument that had been first voiced by illustrious legal expert Tahir Mahmood, who was quoted extensively in the judgment. Mahmood had held that triple talaq was not essential to Islam. In fact, he went a step further to argue that talaq itself was not an essential ingredient of faith.

The judgment by justices Nariman and Lalit, setting aside triple talaq, made it two judges in favour of annulling instant divorce. But there were two votes upholding it too. What tilted the scales in favour of setting aside instant triple talaq was the judgment of Justice Joseph, who struck a balance between the two verdicts, but crucially ruled against instant triple talaq. Calling it un-Islamic and against the sharia, he agreed with Justice Nariman that it was not an essential part of the Muslim Personal Law, but agreed with the Chief Justice on the sanctity of freedom of religion. Though not in agreement with Justice Nariman's viewpoint on the Shariah Act, he stated that since triple talaq is not mentioned in the Quran, it cannot be called a part of the sharia. He wrote:

> The holy Quran has attributed sanctity and permanence to matrimony. However, in extremely unavoidable situations, talaq is permissible. But an attempt for reconciliation, and if it succeeds revocation are the Quranic essential steps before talaq attains finality. In triple talaq this door is closed, hence triple talaq is against the basic tenets of the holy Quran and consequently, it violates Shariat.

Importantly, he did not set aside triple talaq because it was violative of the Constitution, but of the sharia, thereby upholding India's famed pluralism.

Then came about the little tweaking of the famous line on the issue of divorce in Islam, 'What is sinful in theology must be bad in law too'. That is how the five-judge bench set aside instant triple talaq.

At one level, the judgment is a landmark in upholding the sanctity of the Quran in the affairs of Muslims. It was regarded that other sources of law and guidance for a Muslim, including the Hadith, *ijma* or *qiyas*, can only be considered supplementary to the Quran, not contradictory. Triple talaq is considered a sinful but effective way of divorce for followers of Imam Abu Hanifa. The Hanbalis, though, consider it as a single, revocable divorce. This is an opinion shared by the members of the Ahl-e-Hadith sect, as also the Shias. Though regarded as a valid, irrevocable divorce by the Hanafis, instant triple talaq finds no mention in the Quran. The holy book gives a clear process of divorce wherein emphasis is laid on reconciliation and arbitration. Only after all attempts to narrow down differences between a couple fail does a man have the right to pronounce talaq. Further, each pronouncement of talaq has to be separated by at least a month or one menstrual cycle of the wife. The intervening period is like a cooling-off period, wherein the man is given a chance to take back the talaq. This completely removes high-handedness and arbitrariness from the action. Simultaneously, it gives freedom from lifelong suffering with an incompatible partner. It is this emphasis of the Quran that the judgment upholds, be it the minority verdict or the majority verdict. The Quran is considered paramount by the Supreme Court in deciding the ways of life and matrimony of a Muslim.

In fact, contrary to the fears of the ulema, it has always been so. In various judgments passed by the Gauhati High Court, the Delhi High Court, the Bombay High Court and the Madras High Court, the honourable judges have always based their decisions on the Quran rather than on the beliefs of a particular sect. The universal consistency of the Quran has been upheld time and again. In fact, the Supreme Court's decision could well have been a reiteration of the 2008 *Masroor Ahmed vs the State (NCT of Delhi) & Anr.* verdict. This verdict has been quoted by the apex court in its judgment. In the said case, authored by Badar Durrez Ahmed, the court held triple talaq in one sitting as a single, revocable divorce. Similarly, in the Shamim Ara case (2002)—referred to by Justice Joseph too—the Supreme

Court had itself pronounced that talaq is valid only if it follows the process laid down in the scriptures. In effect, it validated talaq as being a step-by-step process, rather than an instant exercise, to dissolve a marriage.

The highest court had an opportunity to examine the constitutional validity of triple talaq twice earlier, much before the Shayara Bano case. In both cases, which date back to the 1990s, it refused to intervene. In 1993, in the *Maharshi Avadhesh vs the Union of India* case, it declined to intervene as the matter pertained to legislative affairs. Maharshi Avadhesh had approached the Supreme Court by writing a writ petition under Article 32 of the Constitution. He prayed for:

> A writ of Mandamus to the respondents to consider the question of enacting a common civil code for all citizens of India; to declare the Muslim Women's (Protection of Rights on Divorce) Act 1986 as void being arbitrary and discriminatory and in violation of Articles 14 and 15 and Articles 44, 38, 39 and 39-A of the Constitution of India.

The apex court dismissed the petition, saying, 'These are all matters for legislature. The court cannot legislate on these matters.'

Later, in the *Ahmedabad Women's Action Group vs the Union of India* case of 1997, the court refrained as the matter pertained to a state policy.

Importantly, in the latest case, the Supreme Court not only invalidated instant triple talaq, but also maintained the sanctity of other forms of divorce. As stated by Justice Nariman and Justice Lalit, 'Triple talaq alone is the subject matter of challenge—other forms of talaq are not . . . It is clear that this form is manifestly arbitrary in the sense that the marital tie can be broken capriciously and whimsically by a Muslim man without any attempt at reconciliation so as to save it.' It protected the Muslim men's right to divorce their wife out of court, thus negating the plea of the Attorney General, Mukul Rohatgi, who had sought a blanket ban on Islamic divorce. Hence, Muslim men continue to enjoy the right given to them by the Quran to effect a divorce through the most preferred or preferred methods, talaq-e-ahsan and talaq-e-hasan, respectively.

Also remaining unaffected are nikah, khula, the women's right to divorce and the method of inheritance. It is a judgment that is fair not just to women but also to men; there are innumerable men who would like to make amends for any hasty pronouncement of divorce when saner counsel prevails. Islam gives them a second chance; the judgment reiterates that.

Millions of women invest in their marriages love, time and care, and deserve to be allowed to remain with their spouse even after a heated exchange or a showdown. The judgment gives both the spouses an opportunity to let bygones be bygones, just as the Quran emphasizes. It protects women's rights and gives them a sense of security in marriage, just as the Quran would like it to be. The judgment seeks to pardon a burst of anger, giving patience a chance to prevail.

Those who still favour instant talaq are victims of a patriarchal mindset: they follow only half of Caliph Umar's administrative ruling. Yes, he did permit instant talaq in certain special circumstances, but he also ordered the public flogging of the men guilty thereof. Today's defenders of instant triple talaq only follow what suits them, not the complete ruling of the second caliph. It bears reiteration that he did not condone instant talaq, just as our Supreme Court has not.

Equally pertinently, thanks to the judgment of Chief Justice Khehar and Justice Abdul Nazeer, and a separate judgment by Justice Joseph, personal laws are considered inviolable. 'Personal law has constitutional protection. This protection is extended to personal law through Article 25 of the Constitution. It needs to be kept in mind that the stature of personal law is that of a fundamental right,' Chief Justice Khehar and Justice Abdul Nazeer said:

> The practice (triple talaq) being a component of 'personal law' has the protection of Article 25 of the Constitution. Religion is a matter of faith, and not of logic. It is not open to a court to accept an egalitarian approach over a practice which constitutes an integral part of religion. The Constitution allows the followers of every religion to follow their beliefs and religious traditions . . . Religion and 'personal law' must be perceived, as it is accepted, by the followers of the faith. And not, how another would like it to be (including self-proclaimed rationalists of

the same faith). Article 25 obliges all constitutional courts to protect 'personal laws' and not to find fault therewith. Interference in matters of 'personal law' is clearly beyond judicial examination.

Their viewpoint was supported by Justice Joseph's separate judgment. In fact, it was this protection granted to personal laws that initially led the All India Muslim Personal Law Board to claim victory in the Supreme Court judgment; the Chief Justice referred to the AIMPLB stand in his verdict too. About two weeks later, at a meeting in Bhopal, members of the AIMPLB decided not to file a review petition in the Supreme Court precisely for this reason. The members understood that despite their opposition, the court had invalidated triple talaq, but were happy that any doors for future interference with personal laws were effectively shut by the Supreme Court.

At another level, though, the Supreme Court failed to address the immediate concerns of the petitioners Shayara Bano, Aafreen Rehman, Ishrat Jahan, Gulshan Parveen and Atiya Sabri. While Bano was given triple talaq through the postal service by her husband, Rehman's grandfather and brother received it from her husband by speed post. Parveen's husband sent her a talaqnama on a Rs 10 stamp paper when she was at her parents' residence. Ishrat Jahan was told 'talaq, talaq, talaq' on the phone by her Dubai-based husband.

The court invalidated triple talaq. However, it did not specify whether these marriages subsisted, or whether these women could go back to their husbands. If their talaq is held invalid, will the women concerned be given maintenance for the period past? And if they do go back to their marital homes, won't they run the risk of being given a fresh divorce by their husbands, this time maybe through the step-by-step method? The judgment also didn't ask the husbands to take them back.

The situation gives rise to multiple questions. If these women want to marry somebody again, and their talaq is held invalid by the court, how do they go about it? Legally, they remain married to the husbands who pronounced instant triple talaq. Also, in each case, the cooling-off or iddat period of three months after the pronouncements is over. In case the estranged spouses are now willing to live together, do they conduct a fresh nikah? But if the husband is unwilling to undergo a fresh nikah, or to take the wife back, what is the status of these petitioners? Is the pronouncement of instant triple talaq to be treated as a final divorce for all practical purposes? Remember, even in talaq-e-ahsan, after the pronouncement of a single divorce, the marriage dissolves after three months in case the divorce is not revoked before that by the husband. Or, if their marriages technically subsist, but the husbands are unwilling to take them back, do these women obtain divorce through khula and regain their single status? These questions need to be answered. Their half-divorced status, like the case of the half-widows in Kashmir, needs to be attended to, perhaps through a fresh round of litigation. Only then can the affected women get some relief.

The proceedings before the judgment also brought in a whiff of fresh air when the secretary of the All India Muslim Personal Law Board, as a respondent, said:

> I say and submit that the All India Muslim Personal Law Board will issue an advisory through its website, publications and social media platforms and thereby advise the persons who perform nikah and request them to do the following: at the time of performing the nikah, the person performing the nikah will advise the bridegroom that in case of differences leading to talaq, the bridegroom shall not pronounce three divorces in one sitting since it is an undesirable practice in Shariat; that at the time of performing nikah, the person performing the nikah will advise both the bridegroom and the bride to incorporate a condition in the nikahnama to exclude resorting to pronouncements of three divorces by her husband in one sitting.

This affidavit marked a small victory for personal reforms emerging from the community. That a high-profile case in the Supreme Court was needed to bring this about says it all. Not everybody was convinced, though, with many recalling that around fifteen years ago, the board had promised to draft a model nikahnama. Unfortunately, the wait is still on.

12

The Women behind the Change

In the mind of the common man, the Supreme Court's judgment in the *Shayara Bano vs the Union of India and Others* case simply prohibits Muslim men from ending their marriages by giving instant triple talaq to their wives. However, if you look a little deeper, you will find that the judgment and the struggle that preceded it represents a whiff of change in society. This was an instance where not only did five women petitioners approach the highest court for relief, but they had support—moral and otherwise—from two Muslim women activists, namely Zakia Soman and Noorjehan Safia Niaz. Interestingly, the same activists were responsible for getting the doors of Mumbai's Haji Ali Dargah thrown open to women a little earlier. While they have not always enjoyed the support of the scriptures, in the case of triple talaq they quoted extensively from the Quran to push home their point that Islam did not sanction such a means of divorce. They went a step further and questioned the abominable

119

practice of halala too. Again, they found that the way it was carried out in India was totally against the letter and spirit of the Quran, that far from empowering a woman, it tends to punish her for her husband's folly.

Together these seven women questioned established mores and practices common to all patriarchal societies beyond the boundaries of religion. In the coming days and years, they may not always get support from the society, they may not always be right in their demands too, but they have forced Muslim men to engage in a dialogue, to reason, to think and to ponder. That is no small achievement. Courtesy this fight, the Quran may just become the centre of a believer's life when resolving all issues relating to civil affairs. Religion may cease to be the monopoly of men.

Zakia Soman

She has lived in times when her grandmother and aunts kept bundles or *potla*s ready in their ancestral home in Kalupur in the walled city of Ahmedabad. It did not strike her initially, but it was a little holdall of sorts, for the community lived in fear of violence, of communal attacks in Ahmedabad. The potlas contained the family's wealth, the family itself ready to flee their home to a 'safer' Muslim ghetto at a moment's notice. Her paternal grandmother and aunts would grab a potla each and begin walking towards Jamalpur at the first news of violence. Indeed, her grandmother's ransacked home is one of the dominant images of Zakia Soman's childhood.

It is experience that has held Zakia in good stead as she pilots the movement for Muslim women's rights. As a co-founder of the BMMA (alongside Noorjehan Safia Niaz), she fought for their right to enter the Haji Ali Dargah in Mumbai. She was among the women who wanted the Supreme Court to scrap instant triple talaq. And she succeeded. The dargah's doors were opened to women a little while ago. It is difficult to believe when one sees her as a leading voice for Muslim women, but Zakia's success stems from having survived years of a troubled marriage, times when she was routinely at the receiving end of an abusive husband's ire, times when she gave up her identity to keep the marriage ticking, times when the violence took physical shape. Ultimately, one day, it ended. It took sixteen years of an unhappy marriage to a management consultant for Zakia to find herself.

She is a Gujarati Muslim woman, born and raised in Ahmedabad. Her father retired as a college principal and her mother was into academics as well. Barely out of her teens, Zakia fell in love with M—she is still careful not to reveal his name in public. Soon, she got married to him against all advice, all norms. Not only was he older to her by twelve years, he was already a divorcee. The sheen of marriage wore off soon; in 1987, within a month of the nikah, she realized she had made a mistake.

'I was naive. I was gullible,' she says. 'I tried my best for sixteen long years for the marriage to work. Within a year of marriage, my child was born and that became my driving force. I felt I must make it work for my child, if not for myself. I made sacrifices of all kinds. I suppressed my feelings, my desires, my likes and dislikes. I thought, I married this man against everybody's wishes, now let me make it work. I danced to his every tune in the hope that it would make him happy and save my marriage and family. He turned out to be an autocratic father. And I continued to put up with total subjugation in the hope that it would change one day. I was like a slave, a prisoner in this man's fiefdom. I had no support system. I had married against everyone's wishes and my husband ensured that I could not reconnect with my family. He controlled every heartbeat and every breath of mine.'

He decided whom she could meet, whom she could speak to, what she could wear, which jokes to laugh at and how many hours she could sleep. Any aberration was met with a physical response.

Zakia recalls, 'There are women who live and die trying to make their marriage work. I was lucky that I could break free after sixteen years.' She had been 'allowed' to pursue higher studies (though she had to pay a price for that), complete her master's in English literature, and then her MPhil. She was 'allowed' to work; first as a subeditor with an English daily, then as a lecturer in a college at Gujarat University, and finally, for a technological education company. But all along, it was her husband who pulled the strings in their marriage and ruled over her life.

The 2002 Gujarat violence changed it all. That is when Zakia saw suffering from close quarters. Women who had

had their homes reduced to ashes, women who had seen their husbands burnt alive, were a picture of grace and dignity even as they picked up the pieces of their lives again in relief camps. They had been attacked by mobs, their homes had been burnt down. But the women did not lose their desire to get justice.

As Zakia worked among them with her husband, supplying food, clothes and medicine, she was shaken by their strength, their ability to forget the immediate tragedy and focus on getting justice by going to the courts, even knocking on the doors of the Parliament. She felt ashamed of herself.

She had an enviable education and decent work experience, but was still not able to find a solution to her abusive marriage. A little later, when the marital violence became even worse—her husband slapped her so hard that he fractured his hand—she took her son Arastu and walked out of her marriage. She went to her sister's place where she spent the next three months or so trying to find her feet again. Her experience at the camps for the riot-affected stood her in good stead. As she picked up the pieces of her life again, she worked in the social sector. She was a prisoner no more. She could breathe free. The autocratic husband was out of the scene. He did try to reconcile, but gave up as soon as Zakia purchased a flat of her own. She had truly arrived as a woman in her own right. She admits, though, that her husband did give her the mahr due to her, Rs 25,000, besides Rs 1 lakh as maintenance and another Rs 50,000 for their son. But for her, it was much more than a question of compensation. She had squandered away the prime of her life in those sixteen years; her child had been denied a happy childhood. At the time of their separation, she felt like shooting her husband dead, then repeating the process to increase his agony.

The formal divorce, however, did not happen in a hurry. Zakia approached Darul Uloom Nadwatul Ulama in Lucknow, where her khula was formalized and she was declared a free woman. A little later, in 2007, she met Soman Nambiar, whom she married in 2008. She had married M of her own free will at the age of twenty-one. She did likewise with Nambiar, for whom too it was a second marriage.

Her first marriage had been a tale of subjugation and oppression in which she suffered emotionally, socially and physically. She suffered alone in the privacy of her home with her son as witness and co-abused. Her middle-class upbringing did not allow her to speak out against the injustice. She found happiness only in her second attempt at matrimony. This union, however, invited huge criticism from patriarchal quarters. The fact that Soman is a Hindu has been used to attack her campaign for Muslim women's rights.

She had a civil marriage. That fact was used to spread the rumour that she had married as per Hindu rites. It is another matter that when Soman met her parents for the first time, he told her father, 'You can call me Somanullah if you like.' But Zakia is not surprised by those attacking her. She says warily, 'They were not there when I was suffering silently for sixteen years, and now they want to intervene in my personal life!'

Later, as she worked on the campaign to get justice for Muslim women afflicted by instant divorce pronounced by capricious husbands, many in the community wondered if she was a Muslim, and if she was a Muslim, how was it that she had a non-Muslim husband. The orthodox elements took her work with a pinch of salt. For all her appeals that divorce should only be allowed according to the procedure outlined in the Quran, Zakia failed to find acceptance among the conservative 'self-appointed representatives' of the community. Of course, all this did not prevent Muslim women, trapped in unhappy circumstances following whimsical divorces, from approaching her for help and guidance.

The membership of her organization has grown consistently. As in 2002, Zakia was there to guide them post 2007. By the time of the Haji Ali Dargah and triple talaq controversies, she had a wealth of experience to fill in the blanks for other brave women, beaten and dispossessed, but not ready to submit. The Haji Ali battle started in 2012 and came to fruition in 2015. The triple talaq case was shorter: Zakia filed the PIL in May 2016 and the Supreme Court ruled against instant triple talaq in August 2017.

Today, Zakia happily counters those who allege an RSS connection and political design to her campaign by pointing to her work before 2007, when she campaigned against the Modi-led BJP government in Gujarat. She is also aware that similar allegations have been levelled against men who have taken on the established forces—their marriages to Muslim women failing to find them greater acceptance.

Noorjehan Safia Niaz

Life was peaceful, routine and largely uneventful for Noorjehan Safia Niaz. She had just completed her master's in social work from the Tata Institute of Social Sciences and was content staying with her family in Dadar, interacting with her neighbours in cosmopolitan Bombay. The Babri Masjid–Ram Janmabhoomi fire, which had reduced many an innocent dream to ashes, however, did not leave her apartment complex untouched. Its repercussions were felt across the country, with communal riots in parts of Uttar Pradesh, Maharashtra, Madhya Pradesh, Rajasthan, etc. Noorjehan, though, was fortunate. Her neighbours, most of them Hindu, stood by her family, telling them not to worry or think of moving to a Muslim locality. One night, when the mob laid siege to her colony, her neighbours actually lied to some rioters, claiming the family had moved out!

Soon, however, as the tension grew and incidents of violence were reported regularly, they advised Noorjehan's parents to move out. The family shifted out for six months before coming back when things were more peaceful.

The demolition of the Babri Masjid and the subsequent riots left Noorjehan shaken and shocked. She realized that something had to be done. 'On 6 December 1992, I became conscious of my Muslim identity,' she often says. Though saddened by the turn of events, Noorjehan went into introspection mode. 'Why was the masjid torn down? Why are minority rights not protected by the people who rule? Should we be doing something as a community to address our issues? What is it that we can do constructively rather than play a victim each time?' she asked herself and plunged headlong into working for the relief and rehabilitation of women affected by the riots.

This passion to work for the exploited consumed her day and night. After working briefly for a state government organization created for the economic upliftment of women, she joined YUVA (Youth for Unity and Voluntary Action) and realized that there was little by way of independence for women in her society, Muslim women included. YUVA mobilized poor urban people on issues that adversely affected them. And Noorjehan worked tirelessly to bring their life back on to an even keel. It was, however, her path-breaking ground-level work in Jogeshwari where she interacted with lower-income-group Muslim families, which shaped her outlook towards religion and society. As she helped marginalized women fight everyday battles, Noorjehan began to appreciate the challenges that lay ahead. That, in turn, led to her founding the BMMA with Zakia Soman, who had also tapped into her reservoirs of inner strength after the 2002 Gujarat violence.

The two of them joined hands to shape the BMMA, which now has more than one lakh members and regularly gets mails from distressed women across the country. So naturally, when Shayara Bano was fighting her case in the Supreme Court, the BMMA came forward to help. Soon, the cases of Aafreen Rehman, Ishrat Jahan and others were linked to the original petition by Shayara Bano.

When the Supreme Court, in a landmark judgment, set aside instant triple talaq, there was jubilation across the country, but also a note of caution for Noorjehan and her colleagues. There was the realization that the court had not said a direct word about the marital status of the petitioners, and that despite the court ruling, it might not be easy to set aside instant talaq in real life.

'I understand the judgment does not address the immediate cause of the five petitioners. We plan to reach out to the legislature to demand codification of the personal law as directed by the Supreme Court. We are satisfied that the court has set aside instant triple talaq, but we had asked for invalidating halala and polygamy too,' Noorjehan states.

One can understand the call for invalidating halala as it finds no mention in the Quran the way it is practised in some quarters. But the Quran does allow a man to take up to four wives, provided he can deal with them with justice and fairness. So, isn't Noorjehan trying to go against the Quran?

'Not at all. The verses allowing men to take up to four wives, but telling them if they cannot deal justly with all four it is better to marry only one, were for a specific time in Islamic history. The defence for polygamy comes from a verse in Surah Nisa. That verse was revealed in specific circumstances and not meant as a blanket permission,' Noorjehan says, defending her decision.

Incidentally, like most Muslim children, Noorjehan learnt to read the Quran in its original Arabic form. But as she did not know Arabic, she never understood its meaning, the rights it conferred on women, the way of life it expected the faithful to follow, etc. It was as an activist that she decided to read an English translation of the Quran. Then she read many an alim's version of the meaning to get a clear understanding of the book. These efforts came about when she was confronted with the problems of Muslim women in Jogeshwari and elsewhere. For their everyday problems, she had to find a solution in the Quran. However, the Hadith often seemed a mountain too high.

'I realized that if I spend not just this life, but even two more lives, I would not be able to read all the Hadith books. Plus, there is always a question of authentic or inauthentic Hadith. So I decided to go back to the original source, the Quran. I read it to understand the powers it has given women. The maulanas do not talk of these powers because we live in a patriarchal society and the maulanas would not want to be challenged.'

During her work with Muslim women, she realized that the feeling of subjugation had been internalized by many of them. When Noorjehan and her colleagues tried to reason with them, many initially refused to believe them, taught as they were since childhood a certain way of religion dictated by men.

For all her brave work, there are insinuations that Noorjehan, along with Zakia Soman, has been propped up by the right-wing government. She counters, 'When is a good time to talk of change, to talk of reforms? If not now, then when? We have waited for seventy years, but nothing has changed. Even the All India Muslim Personal Law Board had a lot of time to bring about change, but all we got were half-hearted measures. The women had to do something themselves. And some of the maulanas are reacting the way they are because they are not able to counter our reasoning. So they indulge in casting aspersions and hurling accusations. But we will not back down. We want Muslim law to be codified.'

Indeed, Noorjehan counts Amina Wadud, the woman who led Friday prayers in the US, as her inspiration. Much before the Supreme Court judgment on triple talaq, Noorjehan and Zakia Soman fought for the rights of Muslim women who sought permission to enter the Haji Ali dargah in Mumbai. And they won. That was an early but notable success. Also notable was Noorjehan's attempt to train Muslim women to be qazis, to apprise them of what the Quran says, what the Sunna of the Prophet says. They set up Darul Uloom Niswaan, a centre for Islamic learning. The centre trains women qazis in the study of the Quran, the Hadith and the sharia. The women are trained to conduct nikah, fill up nikahnamas, etc. Then followed all-women sharia courts, which interpreted religious injunctions in a manner deemed fair to women. Noorjehan and Zakia have now come up with the draft of what is called the Muslim Family

Law. It seeks to establish consistency in the family laws of Muslims.

Soon, the triple talaq judgment followed. 'As women, we are satisfied with the judgment. It upholds the Quranic way of divorce. But there are still battles to be waged, like the plight of women who would be divorced through triple talaq in future. What will their status be? Will their husbands be penalized for it? We want such an action to fall under the Domestic Violence Act,' says Noorjehan. And the fight goes on.

Shayara Bano

Had the qazis of Kashipur in Uttarakhand known better, the nation would not have been witness to the high-voltage triple-talaq drama unfolding before the eyes of eager women and nervous men. That it finally ended with the highest court of the land setting aside instant triple talaq is no mean consolation. However, Shayara Bano, the woman who first petitioned the court, would not have suffered had the imams and qazis she and her father met understood the Quran better and been willing to share the teachings of the book with them. Further, if the qazis of Kashipur knew about the Hanbali ruling (considering triple utterance of the word at the same time as only a revocable divorce), Shayara Bano's marriage could have been saved.

Equally importantly, when Shayara Bano was going through years of abuse and torture at the hands of her husband, she could have been helped had the patriarchal forces of society told her about the right to divorce available to Muslim women. No imam or knowledgeable man told Shayara Bano about khula, under which she could have escaped from the clutches of her husband without even assigning a reason for walking out of the marriage. She could have been saved the public expression of a personal matter, as also the ensuing anguish. Unfortunately, for years, Shayara Bano put up with her property dealer husband's demand for dowry, a car and cash. For years, she underwent abortions. In the absence of any social support, she was reduced to being a helpless soul. A kidney ailment and the absence of medical care at her husband's place in Allahabad forced Shayara Bano to go back to her parents' in Uttarakhand for treatment. It was a small step for Shayara Bano that was to prove a giant leap for womankind.

In Allahabad, she had not heard of khula or even talaq-e-tafweez. In Kashipur, she was to understand the reality of instant talaq and then challenge the patriarchal interpretation of the divorce laws of Islam. The journey from being a meek wife to a bold woman ready to challenge established forces of male hegemony took her almost fourteen years. But before the moment of self-realization, she was dealt a cruel shock. At her parents' house, she received a call from her husband, who informed her that a speed post had been sent to her regarding some property papers. With property talk pretty normal in a property dealer's house, the unsuspecting wife received the packet in October 2015. When she opened it, though, it contained no documents pertaining to property. Instead, there was a talaqnama, with the three dreaded words written clearly. Also attached was a cheque of Rs 15,000—included in it were both her mahr and maintenance for three months. With the receipt of one post, Shayara Bano's life turned upside down. She was no longer a married woman with two kids, but a divorcee who had to fight for the custody of her children. No other maintenance came her way and communication between the former spouses broke down completely, with Shayara Bano unable to even touch base with her children who were residing with their father. Soon afterwards, her husband remarried.

It was at this time that Shayara Bano's father contacted the local alims, qazis and imams to understand the status of her marriage. All of them declared that the marriage was over with the simple sending of the talaqnama and its receipt by the wife. No alim asked her about the school of jurisprudence she or her husband followed. To this day, Shayara Bano does not know if her husband was a Hanafi, where instant talaq is considered valid, or followed the Hanbali ruling, where a single talaq at a sitting followed by multiple pronouncements at the same time was considered a single, revocable divorce. Nor is she certain if she is Hanafi. Asked if she was a Hanbali, she replied, 'I am not sure. I do not know, but we must be Hanafi. Our affidavits declare so.'

This lack of clarity about the school they followed provided ample opportunity to the clerics to consider Shayara Bano's instant talaq as only a single, revocable divorce. A similar case had arisen in the late 1990s, when a British man had raised the subject in front of Islamic scholars at a congregation organized by the Islamic Fiqh Academy (India) in Hyderabad. He had divorced his wife through instant talaq, a procedure similar to the one followed by Shayara Bano's husband, Rizwan Ahmed. He was asked about the imam he followed. Since he did not know whether he was a Hanafi, a Maliki, a Shafi'i or a Hanbali, the scholars concluded that his pronouncement would be considered a single divorce, and he was given the option of revoking it through word or action. The same action in the case of Shayara Bano could have saved her marriage. Notably, even after the Supreme Court ruling rendering instant talaq void, she said, 'I could have considered going back to my husband for the sake of my children. However, he has remarried. Now, it is not possible. I cannot accept it.'

Rizwan has settled down with a new wife. Therein lies the problem. Men marry for pleasure, then pronounce talaq and settle down again with another woman.

Shayara Bano, though, cannot get married again. Not immediately, in any case. The Supreme Court made triple talaq in one sitting invalid. By that yardstick, her marital rights should be restored and she should continue to be Rizwan Ahmed's legally married first wife. But in the absence of directions to the husband to take her back honourably, Shayara Bano is in a no-win situation. Her erstwhile husband does not regard her as his wife any more—before sending her the instant-talaq letter he had filed a case against her, seeking restitution of conjugal rights, as Shayara Bano was staying with her father in

Kashipur. Yet, his pronouncement of divorce is now invalid. For Shayara Bano to marry again, she will have to divorce her husband, that is, obtain khula. Of course, it is also believed by the faithful that since the husband gave her talaq (even if it is regarded only as a single, revocable divorce), the three-month waiting period in which the couple could have reconciled is also over, the talaq is complete. And Shayara Bano, like other petitioners, is free to choose a new partner.

A lack of awareness and clarity marked Shayara Bano's journey from Allahabad to Kashipur to, finally, the Supreme Court in New Delhi. Even when she petitioned the highest court, she sought a ban on unilateral, instant talaq, nikah halala and polygamy. At that stage too, no maulana told her about the true status of halala and polygamy in Islam. There is no nikah halala mentioned in the Quran, the way some clerics insist. And the holy book clearly allows men to have more than one wife. Tell this to Shayara Bano, and she says, 'Yes, there is nothing called halala in the Quran, but nobody told me about polygamy—whether it is allowed by the Quran or not. However, even if a man has more than one wife, he must treat them equally. If he cannot do justice, then it is better to have only one wife. My fight is no longer personal. It is for all women. At one point, I thought of withdrawing the petition when I was told by people that I was going against Islam, and that it would raise a controversy. However, I fought on because I wanted justice in the light of the Quran. Nothing else. No woman should have to go through what I did. My daughter should not have to suffer the way I did. I am fighting to get custodial rights for my children too.'

Aafreen Rehman

Young Aafreen Rehman was going from her brother's residence in Jaipur to meet her *nana* (maternal grandfather) in Jodhpur, accompanied by her mother. The bus she was travelling in collided with a truck. Aafreen sustained fractures in her legs. Her mother died on the spot. Despite a disturbed marriage, her husband arrived to be by her side. For the first time in her married life, he seemed to be caring for her.

After a few days, he went back to Indore, where he was based, promising to be back soon. He never returned. After numerous calls and messages, he blocked Aafreen. Instead, he sent a letter written in Hindi by speed post to her nana in Jodhpur and her *mamun* (maternal uncle) in Jaipur. Both received the post. The same post was sent to her cousin, Naseem Akhtar, too. The cousin refused to receive it. The grandfather and uncle were not as careful. On opening the packet, they discovered it contained the three dreaded words, written by Aafreen's husband, Syed Ashar Ali Warsi, in his own handwriting. Talaq, talaq, talaq.

Aafreen's world, which had never been a bed of roses anyway, came crumbling down with this letter that was received towards the end of January 2016. Her tumultuous marriage, arranged through a matrimonial site in August 2014, was over. Before the receipt of the so-called unilateral talaqnama, Aafreen, an MBA, had put up with sustained torture in the hope of things improving over time, and also because of the realization that her brothers had taken a hefty loan to finance her wedding.

After being married to Warsi, Aafreen moved to Indore. Soon, she got a job as a store manager. However, it was objected to by her mother-in-law, who suggested she pick up a teaching job. Other differences cropped up soon after. Within a few months of marriage, she realized that her family had made a mistake by choosing the lawyer for her husband. He hailed from a reputed family, but he was a wife beater. At the slightest disagreement, he would physically abuse his wife. There were regular demands for more dowry. The husband would beat her up when the demands were not met. About a year after marriage, in August 2015, she was thrown out by her husband, only to be taken back soon after persuasion from Aafreen's brothers and mother—her father had passed away in 2009. Warsi, though, learnt no lesson, and packed her off again in September—this time in an overnight train to Jaipur without a reserved ticket.

After spending a few days with her brother, Aafreen headed to her grandparents' house with her mother. This was to be a fatal journey for her mother, and a calamitous one for Aafreen, who was divorced a few months later through the instant-talaq method.

Aafreen, however, refused to accept the talaqnama without protest. She contacted the local qazi for his opinion on the alleged divorce. The enlightened man held the three talaqs written on a piece of paper invalid. He argued that in the light of the Quran it was not the proper way of ending a marriage as the first stage of reconciliation had not been considered. His ruling, though, had no impact on Aafreen's marriage. However, it did help in bringing about a meeting between the estranged spouses. The couple met once to thrash out issues following the qazi's ruling, but it ended in more threats and humiliation for Aafreen. Her husband refused to take her back. He changed his phone number, blocked her on social media and severed all links with her family. Even a visit to his ancestral place yielded no benefit as Aafreen's family found the house locked.

She, however, refused to give up and lodged a police complaint of domestic violence against Warsi and his mother. They were arrested. But the arrests brought Aafreen no relief. The same day, her brother ended his life. It was too much to take even for Aafreen, who slipped into depression.

However, once again, like the proverbial phoenix, she rose from the ashes of ruined relationships to take her husband on in the court of law.

As she explored her options to hold her husband accountable, she met the volunteers of the BMMA and approached the Supreme Court. The court clubbed her petition with the larger case against instant talaq or triple talaq. As the court set aside instant triple talaq, Aafreen could only say, 'What I have gone through nobody else should have to experience.' Again, though, her joy proved to be temporary. The honourable court had rendered instant talaq void, but had said not a word about her marriage. Nor was there a direction to her husband. The judgment does not talk of maintenance, alimony, etc. Today, if Aafreen wants to marry another man, she might just find herself at a crossroads again. Is her instant talaq valid? Or, if it is considered only a single, revocable divorce, as is the case in many Muslim countries, does she have to marry Warsi again, as the three-month period of iddat is long past? That is, assuming he takes her back after being sent to jail. And if he does not take her back, as is likely, what is Aafreen's marital status? Does she take recourse to khula to marry another man she may choose as her husband? There are more questions than answers in Aafreen's life at the moment. Maybe the answers will come when she approaches the court again for a word on her marital status, maintenance, alimony, etc. She may have won the battle, but the war has to go on.

Ishrat Jahan

'What did Ishrat Jahan gain?' That is the question Ishrat, one of the triple-talaq petitioners, asked herself, and everybody in general, following the Supreme Court judgment invalidating instant talaq. Indeed, as women activists exchanged sweets and political leaders got busy patting themselves on the back, Ishrat Jahan cut a lonely figure. The thirty-two-year-old mother of four kids wondered aloud, 'Everybody is happy. Everybody has welcomed the judgment. The women activists tell us so. Our political leaders say that too. Even our Prime Minister said it will give strength to women. They all say it is good for women. Nobody will be divorced through triple talaq now. But what about me? What has the judgment given me? Any maintenance, any alimony? Nothing. The court banned triple talaq, but it gave me nothing.'

She went on, 'I am still angry. I am still hungry. Two of my children, who had been taken by my husband, have just come back to me. How do I feed them? My husband is happily married. He lives with his wife. Where do I go? Now his family even denies he divorced me. If that is true, how come he did not send me a rupee all these years?'

After the Supreme Court verdict, her husband, Murtaza Ansari, offered to take her back. Ishrat, though, wouldn't have any of it. 'First, his family says he did not divorce me. Now he says he wants me back. I will not go back to him. A man cannot sleep with two women on the same bed,' she said with finality. However, she cannot remarry without getting a divorce from Ansari, or obtaining divorce through khula. 'I will not get married again. To anybody. Why should I? There is no reason,' she declared.

Indeed, Ishrat Jahan's plight is heart-rending. She was married at the age of fourteen to Ansari, a matriculate craftsman from Bihar. He was into embroidery. The couple shifted to Howrah and soon had a daughter. Then another. Then another. By the time the third daughter was born, Ansari had almost given up on his wife. Blaming her for the birth of the girls, Murtaza often inflicted physical violence on her and constantly badgered her for a male heir.

Amid all this, Ishrat managed to clear her class XII examination. And then, after more than a decade of being married, she was blessed with a male child. Too late, as it turned out. Her husband had already decided to marry another woman in his desire for a male child. Ishrat's pleadings had little impact on their ruined relationship. One day, over the phone, Ishrat had a heated exchange with her husband, who was then based in Dubai. He pronounced 'talaq, talaq, talaq' then and there. Ishrat was shocked. Her marriage had fallen apart. She consulted no cleric, no qazi. The divorce hit her hard. 'Who explains things properly? Nobody. I did what I thought was correct,' she said.

But what came along with divorce was worse. Ishrat, with no roof over her head and no source of income, refused to vacate the house she shared with her in-laws. Further, as she claims, there were two attempts at molestation by her brother-in-law. She filed a complaint with the police. No action ensued. She, however, refused to move out. Further, thanks to the support from Nazia Elahi, an activist-lawyer, she lodged a case against her husband for instant talaq without maintenance or mahr in a lower court in Kolkata. She fought all the way to the Supreme Court, where the apex court rendered triple talaq in a single sitting void. It brought her little cheer.

'I have not got a single rupee from my husband as maintenance for the past two-three years since he divorced me in April 2015. I work as a tailor and earn only around Rs 3000 a month. It is not sufficient to feed my children. My sister helps me out,' she says. Ishrat has four children aged between seven and thirteen; two of them stay with Ansari's family and his second wife in Bihar. The two girls with Ansari are maltreated, she claims. Ishrat dearly wants them back. 'But where is the money?' she asks.

If she thought her troubles would be over after the judicial verdict, there was another shock waiting. Unlike Shayara Bano, who was supported by her father, or Aafreen, whose brother and cousin stood up for her, or even Gulshan Parveen, who had her brothers by her side every step of the way, there was no support for Ishrat. Her in-laws blamed her for bringing disrepute to the family by going to court. Her neighbours complained about her conduct and boycotted her. They asked her to move out of the locality. When she refused, she was threatened with more violence and abuse. The verdict may have pleased many, but it left Ishrat homeless and hopeless. 'I could have thought of going back to my husband, but he has another wife. Islam permits a man to marry four women, but one has to take permission. My husband did not even ask me. He just got married. If I go back to him now, as he is suggesting, what is the guarantee he will not throw me out again? And as I have been divorced for more than two years now, I will need to have a nikah again. I will not do that. I will not remarry. I cannot be his second wife now.'

Instead, she has decided to give a new direction to her life by joining politics. Towards the end of 2017, she joined the Bharatiya Janata Party and pledged to work for all women who have suffered. The move may or may not prove to be the anchor she had been hoping for. It did, however, set tongues wagging. Her husband, too, reiterated that he had not divorced her over the phone from Dubai and that she was his wife when she went to court. Ishrat refuses to react. 'People will say what they want. But I have to worry about my children. I cannot keep crying. I cannot hope for my husband to provide for me. I had to make a beginning somewhere. Hopefully, the party will give me a good opportunity to work for the betterment of Muslim women,' she sums up.

Gulshan Parveen

On 22 August 2017, when the Supreme Court invalidated instant triple talaq, Gulshan Parveen, one of the five petitioners, was the only one who expressed a wish to reunite with her husband for the sake of their three-year-old son. 'It will be a sacrifice. The only reason I want to return to my husband is so that my son can grow up in a family,' she said. A month later, her husband was yet to establish any contact with her. As deduced from the Supreme Court judgment, her marriage subsists. But she has been divorced for more than a year—her husband had sent her a talaqnama on a Rs 10 stamp paper when she was at her parents' house in Rampur in western Uttar Pradesh. Gulshan, a postgraduate in English literature, refused to receive it. Soon, her husband approached a family court in Rampur for divorce on the basis of the talaqnama she had refused to receive. However, that was in early 2015. Today, even if one were to regard her instant triple talaq as only a single, revocable divorce, she would need to have a fresh nikah with her husband as the three-month iddat period is long past. Gulshan, though, will have none of it. As her Ghaziabad-based brother Rais Ahmad says, 'We don't consider a piece of paper as evidence of talaq. The wife was not present. Before talaq, there has to be arbitration, the elders have to sit and decide.' Gulshan also reasons, 'When no nikah is complete without the consent of the wife, how can talaq be final without the approval of the wife?' It is a reasoning based on the Hadith, wherein Caliph Umar is said to have asked a woman who had been given triple talaq by her husband if she agreed. It is only when the woman nodded in approval that the talaq was deemed final, and the man subjected to lashes.

In Gulshan's case, after the one-sided divorce, the estranged husband did not send her maintenance, not even for the three-month iddat period. It is something Gulshan's family insists she can do without. 'We do not need a paisa from him. We believe there is no divorce. So the question of mahr or maintenance does not arise.'

They reason that if there is no talaq, there is no need for a fresh nikah, or mahr and maintenance either. Incidentally, Gulshan's husband, who works in a call centre in Noida, has not married again. Nor has Gulshan decided to opt for any other man. She feels her marriage subsists—all that is required is for the husband to take care of his wife and his son. With such wisdom, how did things go wrong?

Well, Rampur-based Gulshan got married in 2013. Her husband's was a typical patriarchal family, in which a woman, even after marriage, had to go back to her parents for treatment in case of illness, or delivery in case of pregnancy. Gulshan too was sent to her father's home when she was pregnant, then again for delivery and recuperation. Incidentally, despite the absence of an explicit demand from the groom's side, she was given a handsome dowry, which included household utility items, clothes and jewellery. It was all tacit, all understood. What was missing was a car. This became a sore point for her husband and in-laws, who demanded she ask her brothers for a car. She refused and was subjected to constant harassment. One day, her husband hit her with an iron rod and threw her out along with her then two-year-old child. And her husband thought that was that.

He had, however, underestimated his wife's mental strength and resilience. She was a teacher who had quit the world of academics to give her marriage a serious shot. Thrown out of her husband's house, she refused to leave. She first went to the local police station. Then she filed a case against her husband for domestic violence and dowry harassment—the husband was soon arrested for demanding dowry and for criminal intimidation. Then, when her husband sent her a talaqnama on a stamp paper, she turned down the letter. Soon, with help from her brothers, she approached the Supreme Court after they got to know of the Shayara Bano case. In the highest court, her petition was clubbed with that of Shayara Bano. In August, she got a verdict that gave her reason to hope. 'I do not want my son to grow up without a father,' she insists, ready to fight another round to reunite with her husband. She gets support from her brother Rais, who reiterates, 'She can marry another man. He too can marry another woman. But the son will not get another father. Or mother.'

Today, she waits for her husband. Gulshan Parveen, who completed her BEd after post-graduation, is jobless and dependent on her brothers. Her spirit, however, is intact. As she told a newspaper soon after the Supreme Court judgment, 'I want to look my husband in the eye, and my in-laws too. They failed to break my spirit.' The fight goes on.

Atiya Sabri

In Islam, a woman is hailed in all her roles. According to a Hadith, *jannah* (paradise) lies at the feet of the mother. As a daughter, she is said to be the key to jannah for her parents. As a wife, she completes half of the faith of her husband. And wherever she goes, she has an identity of her own. Never is she expected to change her name or drop her surname to add that of her husband's. She is an equal partner in the successful running of a home. Yet, reality in a patriarchal society like ours can be cruelly different. For all the injunctions of the Quran and reiteration of numerous Hadiths, social norms remain paramount. Thus, though dowry is almost never asked for in most parts of the country among the community, there is often a tacit understanding, an unsaid but not unexpressed desire for handsome dowry—usually all household utility items, a car and jewellery. In some cases, even cash. That all this flies in the face of Islam bothers only a few. Unfortunately, Atiya Sabri's husband and his family were not among those few, as she discovered to her dismay soon after her marriage to Wajid Ali in 2012.

A resident of Saharanpur in western Uttar Pradesh, Atiya is the quietest of women. She refrained from making any tall claims of victory after the Supreme Court judgment, or even making statements about a reunion with her husband. For her, the triple-talaq case was all about fighting for other women, so that no other woman goes through what she, or her co-petitioners, did. She was fighting for her daughters too, who are not old enough yet to understand the implications of instant triple talaq and the instant suffering it unleashes on an unsuspecting woman.

The mother of two daughters, aged three and four, Atiya too suffered at the hands of her husband for not giving birth to a male child. Like the case of Ishrat Jahan, whose problems mounted after the birth of the third girl child, Atiya's troubles got worse after her second daughter was born. In fact, she claimed that after the birth of the second girl, her husband tried to poison her. She survived only because of the neighbours' timely intervention. They even brokered a temporary peace. It did not last. Based on her allegation, her husband was arrested and Atiya headed to her parents' place.

Incidentally, Atiya too had been married for only a couple of years when trouble started. She had an arranged marriage in 2012. Soon, demands of dowry followed from her husband and his parents. When they demanded Rs 25 lakh, Atiya decided to approach the police. Her husband and in-laws were arrested in December 2015. However, a little before the arrests, in November 2015, her husband sent a talaq letter by speed post to her brother's residence. She was not even told about it. Her husband did not say a word to her. He did not call her up. There was no attempt at arbitration. Dowry not satisfactory, daughter born, divorce effected, deed done. Over.

The husband even got a cleric from Darul Uloom, Deoband, to issue a dictate that the divorce was effective with the receipt of the letter. The cleric did not cross-check Wajid's claims. He ignored the message of Surah Hujurat too, which asks people to cross-check a thing lest they regret it later. Atiya refused to take it lying down. She was neither against Darul Uloom, Deoband, nor against the sharia. All she wanted was the implementation of the teachings of the scriptures in whole, not in part. 'The Shariah says no marriage can be solemnized without both parties' agreement. How can marriage be ended with one person's pronouncement?' she asks. She was better informed about the Hadith than her husband thought. In January 2017, she approached the Supreme Court to invalidate triple talaq as it violated the fundamental rights of a woman. Her petition was clubbed with that of Shayara Bano and others. The court set aside instant triple talaq, but there was no direct word on the status of her marriage. Atiya hopes that the verdict will end the agony of those women who have suffered for no fault of their own.

As for her reunion with Wajid, the chances are bleak. After all, Atiya gave birth to two daughters! But isn't a daughter a key to jannah? Well, for Wajid, that was just a Hadith, read, heard, appreciated. No follow-up. Now Atiya grooms them herself, living up to another Hadith of the Prophet, wherein he signalled to his companions with two fingers held together and said, 'Whosoever has three daughters and rears them well, giving them education, etc., will be with me like these two fingers on the Day of Judgment.' When a companion asked, 'What about those who have only two daughters?' he replied, 'Even those.' Therein lies Atiya's strength, and her struggle.

13

Rulings That Paved the Way

The Supreme Court's decision rendering instant talaq null and void has been hailed as being true to the letter and spirit of the Quran. However, it was not the first such instance of the apex court keeping in mind the complete instruction of the holy book when deciding on cases of divorce involving Muslim couples. Nor was it the first time a court in India had judged triple talaq invalid. There have been instances, as recent as 2008, of a court questioning the legal validity or the Islamic veracity of the act. Of course, there has been the much-talked-about Shamim Ara case earlier, which Justice Joseph Kurian referred to in his judgment on triple talaq. In all the judgments, the courts emphasized the proper, unanimously accepted Islamic way of divorce rather than going by any particular Hadith or sect.

In the *Jiauddin Ahmed vs Anwara Begum* case too—quoted by the Supreme Court in the Shayara Bano case—the Gauhati High Court cited passages from the

Quran on the subject, alongside commentaries by Islamic scholars like Maulana Mohammed Ali and Abdullah Yusuf Ali. It laid particular emphasis on the process of reconciliation given in the book, and quoting Abdullah Yusuf Ali, it called it 'an excellent plan for settling family disputes, without too much publicity or mud-throwing, or resort to the chicaneries of the law. The Latin countries recognize this plan in their legal system. It is a pity that the Muslims do not resort to it universally, as they should'. Hearing the petition, the high court quoted the fact that Islam discourages divorce and urges the spouses to overlook each other's flaws. The judge concluded that there had to be a process of arbitration, an attempt at reconciliation, before proceeding with divorce. In the absence of such a thing, the marriage subsisted, and Anwara Begum was awarded maintenance. It was observed that talaq-e-biddat pronounced by the husband without a reasonable cause, without being preceded by attempts of reconciliation, without the involvement of arbiters with due representation on behalf of the husband and wife, would not lead to a valid divorce.

The verdict was similar in the *Must Rukia Begum vs Abdul Khaliq Laskar* division bench judgment authored by Baharul Islam. The court again went into the nitty-gritty of the divorce procedure in the Quran. In the absence of compliance with the procedure by Laskar, the marriage was held to be subsisting and Rukia Begum was awarded maintenance. This was despite Laskar claiming that he had awarded her triple talaq, and that she was no longer his legally wedded wife. The court, however, held that since

Laskar had not satisfied the court that he had followed the Quranic way of divorce, his marriage subsisted. It reminded Laskar that an arbitrary or whimsical dissolution of marriage was strongly condemned in the Quran. The Supreme Court, perusing the high court verdict, stated the following:

> [The] High Court listed the essential ingredients of a valid talaq under the Muslim law. Firstly, the talaq has to be based on good cause, and must not be at the mere desire, sweet will or whim and caprice of the husband. Secondly, it must not be secret. Thirdly, between the pronouncement and finality, there must be time gap, so that the passions of the parties may calm down and reconciliation may be possible. Fourthly, there has to be a process of arbitration, wherein the arbitrators are the representatives of both the husband and the wife. If the above ingredients do not exist, talaq—divorce— would be invalid.

For these reasons, talaq-e-biddat—the triple talaq pronounced by the respondent-husband Abdul Khaliq Laskar—did not satisfy all the criteria for a valid divorce. Hence, Laskar's marriage to Rukia Begum was regarded as subsisting by the Gauhati High Court.

After this case, the Gauhati High Court (division bench) ruled on similar lines in the *Zeenat Fatema Rashid vs Mohammad Iqbal Anwar* case. Referring to the Laskar and Jiauddin cases, the court once again held, 'A Mohammedan husband cannot divorce his wife at his

whim and caprice . . . A divorce must be for a reasonable
cause and it must be preceded by pre-divorce conference
to arrive at a settlement.' The Madras High Court too
considered divorce to be effective only when it followed
the due process given by Islam. The Bombay High Court
also emphasized the attempt at reconciliation to ward off
possible divorce and drew attention to better modes of
divorce: ahsan and hasan. It held:

> The plea taken by the husband in his written statement
> that he had given talaq at an earlier date shall not
> amount to the dissolution of marriage under the
> Muslim personal law from the date on which such a
> statement was made, unless such a talaq is duly proved
> and it is further proved that it was given by following
> the conditions precedent viz, that of arbitration/
> reconciliation and for valid reasons, and more so when
> the mode of divorce [is] alleged to have been given in
> the Ahsan or Hasan form.

Then, of course, we have the relatively better known
Masroor Ahmed vs The State (NCT of Delhi) and Anr. case
of 2008. This too was a single-judge-bench verdict
authored by Badar Durrez Ahmed, son of late President
Dr Fakhruddin Ali Ahmed. According to many legal
experts, the Supreme Court judgment in the Shayara
Bano case is very close to the ruling in the Masroor Ahmed
case. A close scrutiny of this verdict bears the argument
out. Incidentally, it was also relied upon by Anand Grover,
senior advocate for Zakia Soman, who was added as a party

respondent on the basis of an application filed by her. As in the cases of Shayara Bano and Aafreen Rehman, here too, the wife, Aisha Anjum, alleged that she was harassed for dowry and finally thrown out of her marital home. As in Bano's case, Anjum's husband Masroor Ahmed too filed a plea for restitution of conjugal rights after his wife started staying at her paternal home. It is, however, in ruling on the triple talaq—which was pronounced by Masroor Ahmed to his wife Aisha Anjum—that the Delhi High Court delved into the intricacies of talaq.

It stated, and this again was quoted by the Supreme Court:

> There is no difficulty with ahsan talaq or hasan talaq. Both have legal recognition under all *fiqh* schools, Sunni or Shia. The difficulty lies with triple talaq, which is classed as biddat (an innovation). Generally speaking, the Shia schools do not recognize triple talaq as valid divorce. There is, however, difference of opinion even within the Sunni schools as to whether the triple talaq should be treated as three talaqs, irrevocably bringing to an end the marital relationship, or as one *rajai* (revocable) talaq, operating in much the same way as ahsan talaq.

The Delhi High Court concluded:

> It is accepted by all schools of law that talaq-e-biddat is sinful. Yet some schools regard it as valid. Courts in India have held it to be valid. The expression—bad in

theology but valid in law—is often used in this context.
The fact remains that it is considered to be sinful. It was
deprecated by Prophet Muhammad. It is definitely not
recommended or even approved by any school. It is not
even considered to be a valid divorce by Shia schools.
There are views even amongst the Sunni schools that the
triple talaq pronounced in one go would not be regarded
as three talaqs but only as one. Judicial notice can be taken
of the fact that the harsh abruptness of triple talaq has
brought about extreme misery to the divorced women
and even to the men who are left with no chance to undo
the wrong or any scope to bring about a reconciliation.
It is an innovation which may have served a purpose at a
particular point of time in history, but if it is rooted out
such a move would not be contrary to any basic tenet of
Islam or the Quran or any ruling of Prophet Muhammad.
In this background, I would hold that a triple talaq (talaq-
e-biddat), even for Sunni Muslims be regarded as one
revocable divorce. This would enable the husband to
have time to think and to have ample opportunity to
revoke the same during the iddat period. All this while,
the family members of the spouses could make sincere
efforts at bringing about a reconciliation. Moreover, even
if the iddat period expires and the talaq can no longer be
revoked as a consequence of it, the estranged couple still
has an opportunity to re-enter matrimony by contracting
a fresh nikah on fresh terms of mahr, etc.

Then we had the *Nazeer vs Shameema* case (a single-bench
judgment authored by A. Muhammad Mustaque). It was

a case remarkably different from other triple-talaq cases brought before various courts. Here, the spouse/spouses wanted deletion of their former spouse's name from their passport. However, the passport authorities had refused to consider a private, unauthenticated talaqnama as a valid document for divorce. Through interim directions, the high court ordered the passport authorities to correct the spouse details (as were sought) based on the admission of the corresponding spouse that their matrimonial alliance had been dissolved. Though instant talaq was not the direct issue here, the judge noted that 'it requires a state intervention by way of legislation to regulate triple talaq in India.' It further stated, 'The entire exercise in this judgment is to alert the state that justice has become elusive to the Muslim woman and the remedy thereof lies in codification of the law of divorce.'

Both the Masroor Ahmed and Nazeer judgments were referred to by Grover to buttress his contention that talaq-e-biddat was totally unjustified. He urged the court to declare it as illegal, ineffective and having no validity in law, just like the Gauhati High Court and the Delhi High Court had held. Interestingly, Nitya Ramakrishna, the counsel for Noorjehan Safia Niaz, another respondent in the Shayara Bano case, did not ask the court to strike down talaq-e-biddat, but said that it would suffice if it were to merely uphold the order passed by the Delhi High Court in the Masroor Ahmed case.

Back in 2002, in the *Dagdu Pathan vs Rahimbi Dagdu Pathan* case, the Aurangabad bench verdict of the Bombay High Court was often used in the context of instant-talaq cases. In this case, Pathan had submitted before the court that he had divorced his wife in front of a qazi and two witnesses, one of them a Muslim and the other a Hindu. Beyond having a difference of opinion with his wife, and the latter insulting her husband and his mother, Pathan did not cite any other reason for pronouncing talaq. The Aurangabad bench invalidated the instant triple talaq saying, 'To divorce the wife without reason, only to harm her or to avenge her for resisting the husband's unlawful demands, and to divorce her in violation of the procedure prescribed by the Shariat is haraam (forbidden).'

The court declared that a Muslim husband had to follow the stages outlined by the Quran with regard to matters of divorce. The husband was required to give reasons; he had to explain that an attempt had been made at reconciliation through arbitration and third-party counsel, and that it was after the failure of all attempts at peace that he had taken recourse to divorce. The Aurangabad bench verdict was almost a reiteration of the Calcutta High Court judgment in the Chand Bi case.

This case did not hit the headlines, though. What did was the *Shamim Ara vs the State of UP* case. In this instance, the Supreme Court invalidated triple talaq. It held that for a talaq to be considered valid, it had to be pronounced according to the method given in the Quran, that is, in three separate sittings, each sitting separated by a menstrual cycle. It held that to be valid, talaq has to be pronounced as per the Quranic injunction. It was also stated that for talaq to be effective, it had to be for a reasonable cause, and it must be preceded by an attempt at reconciliation. Incidentally, the Prophet himself warned against divorcing one's wife on the basis of mere whim or caprice. He is believed to have said, 'The curse of God rests on he who repudiates his wife capriciously.'

Invalidating triple talaq, the apex court said:

> None of the ancient holy books or scriptures mention such a form of divorce. No such text has been brought to our notice which provides that a recital in any document, incorporating a statement by the husband that he has divorced his wife could be an effective divorce on the date on which the wife learns of such a statement contained in an affidavit or pleading served on her.

In the Shamim Ara case, Justice R.C. Lahoti clarified that a talaq had to be pronounced, as in to 'proclaim . . . formally utter'. Incidentally, the court had then too referred to the *Jiauddin Ahmed vs Anwara Begum* case, as also the *Rukia Begum vs Abdul Khaliq Laskar* case. As in those cases, the court drew generously from the Quran and agreed with the judgments, saying, 'We are in respectful agreement with the . . . observations made by the learned judges of the High Court.'

14

AIMPLB's Points of Action

The All India Muslim Personal Law Board (AIMPLB) is often criticized for obfuscation and oscillation. The non-constitutional body is peopled by men who are not necessarily scholars of Islam. Many are linked to political parties and inevitably have an axe to grind. Only a handful of them are devoted to the cause of Islam. They too have to balance time between their respective parent bodies, like the Jamiat Ulema-e-Hind or the Jamaat-e-Islami and the AIMPLB. In the public mind, the AIMPLB often comes across as an upholder of tradition and conservatism, a body that does little to uplift the community and provides ample fuel to detractors. In fact, its critics allege that the body is opposed to progress, and in particular, to denying women their due.

Of course, like all allegations, there is not always enough substance to back these up. However, AIMPLB members too would admit that they need to be more proactive when it comes to safeguarding women's interests in a patriarchal society. Challenged by women, the body has often equivocated and, at others times, sought to digress from the subject. In fact, some of its former members criticize the board for its lacklustre ways, lack of insight and an inability to interpret Islam in the light of modern-day challenges.

Yet, the way some of the hearings went in the Supreme Court shows the body might just be ready to turn the corner. For once, the board was ready to walk with those whose understanding of Islam or whose interpretation of the word of the Quran might be at variance with its own. It was ready to go by the letter and spirit of the Quran rather than merely taking refuge in homilies. The board's pledge, through an affidavit, that it would issue an advisory against instant triple talaq on its website and other publications was a welcome step, as was its call for a social boycott of those who end their marriage through the pronouncement of instant triple talaq. It did not forget to remind everybody that social boycott works, giving the example of Mewat where the local panchayat called for boycotting those who gave instant triple talaq to end a marriage. Not to be trifled with was a suggestion to qazis to incorporate into the nikahnama a clause that if things did not work out, the couple shall not go in for instant divorce. This was said explicitly. What was implicit was that the board was ready to go against unilateral, arbitrary announcement of talaq by men.

Many openly doubted the board's ability to get its suggestion implemented. And indeed, that is open to question. Yet, the fact that the body could get around 4.8 crore Muslim men and women to sign in its favour shows that it has lost none of its appeal among the common people.

It is, however, the board's eight-step code which instils the hope that the future might just be better, more secure and peaceful for women in particular and the men in general. While detailing the code, the board essentially repeats what the Quran says, emphasizing the process of arbitration and reconciliation.

The board notes through its guidelines that it expects:

Indian Muslims to ensure that they will practise the Islamic Shariat in matters of divorce. The marriage is a permanent and durable kind of relationship but sometime such a situation arises where the relations between the husband and wife become so serious that indwelling becomes impossible. In such a situation separation becomes an inevitable option. But every effort should be made for the betterment of relations before any decision is taken.

It issues an eight-point guideline to spouses:

1. If there are differences between spouses, they should try to resolve these mutually. They must keep in mind that everyone has some bad but many good qualities as well. Keeping in mind the provisions of the Shariat, one must overlook the mistakes of others.

In other words, the spouses are supposed to show a spirit of togetherness rather than alienation and try to sort out their issues in private. They are to act like garments to each other, not expose the partner to public ridicule.

2. If these efforts fail, there may be temporary withdrawal. It could be used to reignite passion for each other, leading to natural conciliation.

3. In case these two steps fail, sincere members of the families concerned, or one arbiter from each family, may be appointed for resolution of differences. They have to try and reconcile the differences and help the couple arrive at a mutually beneficial relationship.

4. If the dispute remains unresolved, the husband may pronounce only one talaq during the period of purity of the wife and leave her till the waiting time ends. If a favourable situation occurs during the waiting period, the husband should retain her and both should continue to be spouses. The divorce can be annulled by saying as much or experiencing intimacy again. If the husband does not retain her, then the marriage automatically ends at the conclusion of the waiting period. If the wife is pregnant during the waiting period, the period shall end only with the delivery of the child. The husband has to incur expenses during the waiting period. In case the mahr has not been paid, it has to be paid during the waiting period.

5. If they reach any amicable settlement after the period of waiting or iddat, they may restore their relationship by undertaking a fresh nikah with mutual consent and a new mahr.

6. The second option is that the husband should pronounce one divorce during the period of purity, then another in the second month followed by the third in the third month. If they reach any amicable decision before the third pronouncement, the husband has to retain her and restore the marriage.

7. In case the wife is not willing to live with the husband, she can opt out with khula.

8. The Muslim community should socially boycott those who are found guilty of pronouncing three divorces in one sitting.

The board also issued an advisory to qazis:

> At the time of performing nikah, the person performing the nikah will advise the bridegroom that in case of differences leading to talaq, the bridegroom shall not pronounce three divorces in one sitting since it is an undesirable practice in Shariat; that at the time of performing nikah, the person performing the nikah will advise both the bridegroom and the bride to incorporate a condition in the nikahnama to exclude resorting to pronouncement of three divorces by her husband in one sitting.

Crucially, the board reiterated that pronouncement of divorce without a reason, or three divorces in one go, is not the sharia-approved method of divorce. It pledged to start a public movement to tell the multitudes to avoid pronouncing divorce for frivolous reasons, and in case of necessity only one divorce should be resorted to.

The words are all there, and almost all of them are derived from the verses and the message of the Quran. No well-meaning soul can dispute a point from the eight-point advice given to couples. What has to be tested still is the sincerity of intent and the follow-up action. How far will the board go to come up with a nikahnama that includes the precondition of no instant triple talaq? How far will it boycott those who have been guilty of triple talaq? How will it advise qazis not to solemnize a nikah where sharia is made a mockery of? Only that action will decide whether the AIMPLB becomes an upholder of justice and fair play, or whether it is reduced to just another NGO using religion to serve its ends. The ball, at the moment, is in the board's court. Time is ticking.

15

No to Instant Talaq in Muslim Countries

A few years ago, writing in his book *Concerning Divorce*, noted Islamic scholar Maulana Wahiduddin Khan said:

> A man may say talaq to his wife three times in a row, in contravention of the Shariah's prescribed method, thereby committing a sin, but if he was known to be in an emotionally overwrought state at the time, his act may be considered a mere absurdity arising out of human weakness. His three utterances of the word talaq may be taken as an expression of the intensity of his emotions and thus the equivalent of only one such utterance.

As the campaign for a ban on triple talaq gathered momentum in 2016–17, it was pointed out, with complete justification, that the practice of instant talaq had been rendered invalid in more than twenty Muslim countries. What was left unsaid was that if a similar thing happened in India, it would not be tantamount to interference in the personal laws of the community, or even infringing upon its rights as a minority. However, what was never pointed out was that these countries' laws were not a monolith. Each country had arrived at its own interpretation of Quranic injunction on the process of possible conciliation that has to precede talaq. Some involved the state, others brought in the families of the spouses. Also, each country looked at a man's right to divorce his wife differently. In some states, the man had to give a written application to the concerned authorities about his intention, following which the state deputed officials to interact with the man and his wife to try and avoid divorce. Importantly, no Muslim country considered the man's right to divorce his wife as a unilateral right, one for which he was not answerable to anybody and which he could exercise at his own sweet whim or fancy. Nowhere did Muslim women live with the fear of instant talaq following any heated exchange or difference of opinion with their husbands. A dish gone wrong or a shirt not ironed well did not result in a divorce. In fact, all countries rendered divorce pronounced in a fit of rage or under the influence of liquor as invalid. Though countries from Tunisia, Libya and Egypt in Africa to Jordan, Saudi Arabia, Kuwait and the UAE in west Asia consider multiple pronouncements of divorce at the same time as nothing more than a single, revocable divorce, the best law on the subject comes from a non-Muslim country. Islamic jurists agree that the changes Sri Lanka made to the process of divorce for Muslims on the island nation are by far the best and very much in consonance with Islamic law.

In countries with a predominance of Muslims, there have been various interpretations of the Quranic laws of divorce, but there has been a consistent attempt at making talaq less of an out-of-court, individual decision. Simultaneously, an attempt has been made to factor in the voice of women, mitigating the psychological and economic impact of divorce on them. When the husband is asked to submit an application to the concerned authority before going in for a divorce, the idea is not to belittle his status as the qawam or head of the family, but to protect the family, which may include small children. To use modern parlance, it is family first; individual whims and anger come much later.

Simultaneously, instances of khula are growing worldwide. Interestingly, while triple talaq in one go has been respected as a legitimate mode of ending marriage by the Hanafis, it is in areas where the Hanafis are either in a majority or in sizeable numbers that the grounds on which a woman may seek to end her marriage through khula have been expanded. These range from the husband's unexplained disappearance, inflicting injury on the spouse, i.e., domestic violence perpetrated by the man and his inability to fulfil marital obligations. Marital infidelity is also among the grounds on which a woman can seek an end to marriage. This includes the partner developing a homosexual relationship as well. Also included is the spouse having, or developing, a chronic illness preventing him from fulfilling his sexual responsibilities. A country like the UAE even includes the condition of HIV as grounds for divorce mooted by the wife. In such cases, no attempt is made to reconcile the couple to prevent any possible transmission of the disease.

Egypt

For centuries, Egypt has been respected in Islamic circles for its universities and scholars. In the subcontinent, too, if an Islamic scholar studied in Cairo he was more easily accepted. It is interesting then that Egypt was probably the first Muslim country to reform its divorce laws, as early as 1929. It did so by following the ruling of Ibn Taimiyah, who believed that multiple pronouncements of divorce without any gap for rethinking or reconciliation stood only for a single divorce. After a man pronounced talaq, whether singular or multiple, the couple was given a ninety-day period to explore avenues of togetherness and to cohabit. In case the man decided to take back his divorce within this period, he could do so either through word or action. No fresh nikah was necessary. For a final divorce, a man had to give divorce at a gap of at least one menstrual cycle. Each pronouncement had to be made when the woman was in a state of tuhr and the couple had not had a physical relationship during that time. After the third pronouncement, the man and woman ceased to be husband and wife, with each free to choose a new partner. So talaq became a three-step process. Importantly, Egypt does not have a majority of Hanafis. Most citizens are followers of Imam Shafi'i.

In 2000, Egypt provided for judicial khula. This was in addition to out-of-court khula or divorce at the wife's initiative. In out-of-court khula, where third parties or arbiters often prevailed upon the husband to accept the khula, the women usually gave away a part of their mahr. However, there were cases in which the husband dilly-dallied to harass the wife. The 2000 ruling gave women statutory power to insist on khula, with men having no power to refuse or delay. Khula became a unilateral right of the wife. The husband's consent was rendered superfluous. In return for her freedom from wedlock, the wife was supposed to waive off any financial rights on her husband. This was like a female counterpart to the man's power of talaq, where a husband could divorce his wife without assigning any reason and against her will. It only involved the payment of mahr and maintenance. Here, a woman too was not required to give a reason for divorce. She just had to forgo financial claims on the husband and return a part of the dower, if already paid. This judicial khula was greeted with derision by the patriarchal society, with many arguing that it went against the concept of men as the leader of women.

Syria

War-torn Syria has occupied a unique place in Islamic history. In fact, according to a version accepted by people who believe in instant talaq, it is said that during the time of Caliph Umar, when Arab men came in contact with Syrian and Egyptian women, they were so overwhelmed by their beauty that they pronounced instant triple talaq on their wives to marry these women. While it is an interpretation that is often contested, the fact remains that Syria, with its mix of Arab, Turkish and Kurdish ethnicities, and a population where almost every fourth person is a Shia, has not been in favour of instant talaq. It is important to reiterate that Shias do not hold instant triple talaq as valid. In Syria, the system of divorce was reformed in 1953, and any number of talaq pronouncements at one and the same time counted only as a revocable divorce, except, of course, when a man did it for the third time—each occasion being separated by at least a month.

Jordan

In the secular state of Jordan, too, triple divorce in one go is outlawed. The state's law is in consonance with the Quranic injunctions on the subject of divorce. Jordan requires registration of divorce in court. There are severe penalties for failing to do so within the specified period. Till 1976, divorce came into effect only after registration with the competent authorities. Since then, a bureaucratic process has been set in motion to discourage the use of triple talaq. Divorce in a state of extreme anger or bewilderment is not held valid.

On khula, too, it is inclined to favour the diminution of a man's role. Its 2001 rule, amended in 2003, is modelled along the lines of the Egyptian rule on the subject. It ruled that the wife has the right to handle her own divorce if it was mentioned in the nikahnama. That is, talaq-e-tafweez, where the husband had delegated his power of divorce to her at the time of nikah. The provision of judicial khula, where the husband's consent was rendered unnecessary, was widely criticized in patriarchal society as being damaging to the family system. However, the provision continued as it was argued that only women suffering in incompatible marriages would choose an expeditious divorce. It also meant that the intimate details of incompatibility were kept out of the public sphere as the woman was not required to explain the reasons for khula.

Kuwait

A theocratic, Sunni-dominated state, Kuwait makes divorce valid only if it is pronounced by a sane adult man conscious of the action and its repercussions. No divorce takes place if the husband is under the influence of liquor or mentally unsound, or if he is angry enough for it to affect his speech and actions. Here, divorce takes place under Law 51 of the Code of Personal Status, 1984.

Kuwait too regards instant triple talaq invalid. It holds that any pronouncement of talaq followed by any number of reiterations shall be considered only a single divorce.

Sudan

While the constitution of Syria's populace resembles that of the Indian populace, where Sunnis are the overwhelming majority but Shias too are sizeable in number, India's case bears the closest resemblance to

Sudan's. In the African country, Hanafi Muslims are in a majority, much like in India. However, unlike in India, there the divorce laws were framed way back in 1935. And just as it was demanded in India before the Supreme Court judgment in August 2017, in Sudan, the divorce laws clearly made talaq a time-consuming affair, and not an instant one. According to Article 3, Shariah Circular No. 41/1935 of Sudan, all divorces by a husband are revocable except the third one. There is one exception to the rule: instances where the marriage has not been consummated, instant and immediate talaq is considered appropriate. This is done to help the woman find a new partner and settle down quickly and not pay any price for marrying a man who might not be capable of discharging his marital responsibilities.

Tunisia

Not often at the forefront of discussion around Islamic countries in this part of the world, Tunisia has made it a bit difficult for a husband to divorce his wife. According to the country's Code of Personal Status, 1956, a husband cannot unilaterally divorce his wife verbally. He has to consult a judge and explain the reasons for it. Thus, marriage—and divorce—is not regarded as a merely individual act. Here, the state comes into play and all divorce proceedings take place before a judge. Also, at the first stage itself, there is a court-directed attempt at reconciliation. An individual's divorce is a state-operated affair, with Article 30 of the Tunisian Code of Personal

Status clearly stating that divorce pronounced outside a court of law will have no validity or effect.

Iraq

A Shia-dominated state, Iraq rejects triple talaq in a single sitting. According to Iraq's personal law, 'three verbal or gestural repudiations pronounced at once will count as only one divorce'. This leaves the door open for spouses to think, ponder and patch up. The law requires the husband to petition the state in case he wants to effect a divorce, but permits him to do so without prior information if he intimates the authorities within the iddat period of three months. The marriage is valid till formal cancellation of the divorce by the court. The court can investigate the reason for trouble in the marriage and appoint arbiters for reconciliation. During the late 1950s, Iraq became the first Muslim country to replace the age-old sharia courts with government-run personal status courts. Pertinently, the 1959 Iraq Law of Personal Status clearly put men and women on an equal footing by stating that 'both spouses have the right to ask for separation when a dissension arises between them, whether before or after consummation.'

In the 1970s, this formal recognition of divorce by the courts was done away with. In Iraq, a woman can seek divorce on the grounds of the husband indulging in gambling, drinking or developing an illness that prevents him from fulfilling his sexual responsibilities. She can also claim divorce if she has no child from him due to his infertility.

Malaysia

Any man or woman who wants to divorce his/her spouse has to give an application to the court in Malaysia. All details of the family, financial status, children, their age, etc. have to be provided. Also, the reasons for filing for divorce have to be explained. The candidate also has to clarify if steps towards reconciliation have been explored. Upon receipt of the application, the court issues summons to the other party, attaching with it the original application form. If the wife (as is usually the case) agrees to the divorce, then one talaq is registered with the court. If the wife contests the husband's decision, the court appoints a conciliatory committee consisting of a religious officer as a chairman, with a representative each from the husband and wife's side. Here, an attempt is made to include the close relatives of the spouses on the committee. The committee is given six months to try a process of reconciliation. If the committee fails to bring about a reconciliation or resumption of the conjugal relationship, it advises the court accordingly. The court then permits the husband to pronounce one talaq. The talaq becomes effective from that date, provided the wife is not pregnant. In case she is, the pregnancy has to end first.

It may be noted that Malaysia is a Sunni-dominated country. The role of the conciliatory committee, however, is done away with in case either of the spouses suffer from an incurable mental illness, or one of the spouses is imprisoned for a minimum of three years.

Sri Lanka

The island nation involves the qazi, and also the families of the parties concerned, in a divorce. All attempts are made at exploring options of reconciliation between the spouses. It's not just a talk between the spouses— even the neighbours and other influential people are involved in an attempt to discourage divorce. According to Sri Lanka's Marriage and Divorce (Muslim) Act, 1951, which was subsequently amended in 2006, a husband planning to divorce his wife has to notify the qazi. The qazi, in turn, involves the spouses' family and influential elders to bring about rapprochement. This process takes a month. However, at the conclusion of the month, and of all attempts at reconciliation, a man can give talaq to his wife in the presence of the qazi and two other witnesses. Islamic scholars believe that in the Indian subcontinent, the Sri Lankan Divorce Act is the closest to the letter and spirit of the Quran. It may be recalled that the Quran too asks the spouses to try and sort out differences, failing which, they are instructed to call two witnesses, one from each side. Only after exhausting all avenues to bring about peace can a husband divorce his wife.

Pakistan and Bangladesh

Both Pakistan and Bangladesh are Sunni-majority countries. Also, both have a sizeable number of followers of Imam Abu Hanifa. This should translate into acceptance of instant triple talaq. However, it does not. Both countries have a clear process through which spouses can end their marriage. Instant triple talaq is not an option. The change has come about despite opposition from the well-entrenched patriarchal forces, opposed to a law that they see as tantamount to diminution of their authority. Aberrations are reported to this day, but the law prohibiting instant triple talaq is in force.

Pakistan has the Muslim Family Law Ordinance Act (MFLO), 1961, to guide the nation. This law also came about after sustained agitation by women, and the action of the State to arrive at unanimity. The rules governing the abolition of triple talaq were formulated based on the recommendations of a seven-member commission on marriage and family laws, which was set up in 1955. The commission had three common citizens as members, besides one Islamic scholar. There were three members— Begum Anwar G. Ahmad, Begum Shamsunnahar Mahmood and Begum Shahnawaz—from the All Pakistan Women's Association, which had set in motion the campaign against bigamy. Interestingly, the campaign started against Prime Minister Muhammad Ali Bogra, who had married his secretary even though he had a legally wedded wife. Surrendering to the demands of the activists, the government set up a seven-member commission for matters of marriage and family laws. The commission was authorized to report on 'the proper registration of marriages and divorces, the right to divorce exercisable by either partner through a court or by other judicial means, maintenance and the establishment of special courts to deal expeditiously with cases affecting women's rights.'

The commission recommended that three divorces at one time would effectively be a single divorce. For a final, irrevocable divorce, two further announcements had to be made by the husband at the conclusion of the wife's menstrual cycle, in her pure period, during which no physical relationship between the spouses should have been established. The members also insisted that a person desirous of divorcing his wife would need to obtain an order to that effect from a family or matrimonial court.

The conclusions of the commission were met with social and political criticism across the country, with the clerics in particular questioning the credentials of some of the members and alleging that their suggestions went against the sharia. They were especially against the need to obtain a court permit for pronouncing divorce; they felt the state was entering people's bedrooms, and that how or why a man ended his marriage should remain between the partners. A member of the commission, Maulana Thanvi, objected to the commission's conclusions with a dissenting note of his own. He argued:

> To put a restriction on the exercise of this right by making it ineffective if talaq is not registered or not authorized by the matrimonial and family laws court, not only amounts to tampering with the injunctions of the faith but also putting obstacles in the way of dissolution even when it becomes necessary and desirable.

Trying to strike a balance, the MFLO, 1961, ruled that any man desirous of divorcing his wife shall inform the chairman of the Union Council in writing. He, however, was allowed to do so immediately after the pronouncement of talaq, and not necessarily before uttering the words. Thus, a man could divorce his wife out of court, but had to inform the authorities in writing immediately. His failure to do so left him open to punishment, which could include a fine of Rs 5000 and/or simple imprisonment for a term that may extend up to a year.

Also, it was noted that a talaq, unless revoked earlier through word or action, was not effective until the end of ninety days from the date of receipt of the application/notice at the chairman's office. The chairman, in turn, constituted an arbitration council to attempt a possible rapprochement between the spouses. If the ninety-day period ended and the husband failed to revoke talaq, he could marry his wife again if she was willing, with no third-party intervention. This option was not available after the third and final divorce.

The country was faced with a controversy on the issue of the failure of the man to inform the Union Council's chairman about his plan to give talaq. While a section of the ulema still considered the talaq valid, most activists believed that the marriage, not divorce, was valid. The latter held that the marriage subsisted till the submission of the application. As late as 2012, Pakistan's popular English daily *Dawn* reported a controversy arising out of the MFLO. In this instance, the newspaper reported that one Hamid Mughal accused his wife, Tahira Naseer, of bigamy. It was alleged that Tahira married Naseer Mehmood Khan in August 2000. Less than a year later, in June 2001, Naseer divorced his wife through the instant-talaq method.

Believing that she had been legally divorced, Tahira went back to her parental place. In January 2003, she married Hamid Mughal in Pakistan. Later, the marriage ceremony was conducted in Fairfax, Virginia, USA. On the court documents, Tahira claimed that she was not earlier married and that Hamid Mughal was her first husband. The couple had differences, but continued to live in the USA. However, a chance trip by Mughal to Pakistan in 2009 revealed that Tahira had been married earlier, to Naseer. He happened to stumble upon her marriage certificate, and soon returned to the USA to sue his wife for bigamy. Tahira protested that she was not married to Naseer any more, and that she had been divorced by him through three pronouncements of talaq at one time. The MFLO, however, invalidated instant talaq. Also, it made it necessary for even a single pronouncement to be reported to the concerned authority as soon as possible. In this case, Tahira's first husband, Naseer, was not only guilty of pronouncing instant talaq, but had also failed to back it up by informing the authorities concerned. Had he done so, his divorce would have been considered revocable within ninety days.

Tahira, for no fault of hers, could be accused of bigamy, and worse, of adultery in Pakistan. In Virginia, too, her husband was able to turn to the hardly used provision of the MFLO to get the marriage annulled rather than pay mahr and maintenance, which would have ensued in case of talaq.

Her case was similar to the one involving Shahida Parveen and Mohammed Sarwar that made headlines in 1988.

Incidentally, Bangladesh, which was carved out of Pakistan in 1971, inherited the MFLO. Here, one issue was discussed threadbare. A man gives talaq and follows it up with a notice to the chairman of the Union Council. The council is then required to set up a conciliation committee. However, if it fails to set up the committee, or if the committee fails to give its verdict within ninety days, will the talaq pronounced by the husband be effective? The court ruled that the divorce would be effective at the end of ninety days from the receipt of the notice. Interestingly, unlike in Pakistan, in Bangladesh the high court division ruled, in the *Mohammed Kutubuddin Jagirdar vs Nurjahan Begum* (1973) case, that sending a notice to the chairman and to the wife is a prerequisite for the validation of divorce.

16

Instant Triple Talaq and Khula in Qazi Courts

In the last quarter of 2017, preparations were under way to get Darul Qaza up and running on Mira Road in Maharashtra's Thane district. Queries had been coming in from local Muslims if the latest addition to the AIMPLB's stream of local Islamic courts would consider instant triple talaq as a single, revocable talaq, or as a final, irrevocable divorce. Marriage over, case shut. There would be no decision that would go against the teachings of the Quran or the Sunna, they were assured. Whether it translates into a yes or no to instant triple talaq is open to interpretation.

A clue, however, comes from the thought process and decisions of another Darul Qaza court on Nagpada Road in Mumbai. Every month, the Nagpada outlet gets up to twenty cases of talaq. In most cases, the husband approaches the court. The Darul Qaza clerics, though, are successful in bringing about a rapprochement in most cases, claiming that up to fifteen cases are resolved through reconciliation, negotiation and consultation. The involvement of the qazi, along with some family elders, is beneficial. Divorce, the most hateful of things allowed in Islam, is thus prevented.

The remaining cases, however, result in divorce which is also, at times, delayed to give peace a second chance. In cases where the husband has pronounced only one divorce, efforts are usually successful at smoothening out differences and bringing the parties together during the subsequent three-month iddat period. However, where the husband utters the dreaded word thrice, the clerics are only approached to give the divorce certificate or issue a fatwa that the man and woman cease to be husband and wife from a given date. In most such instances, the parties get married again within six months to a year. In the rare case that they do not want to make amends, the qazi considers it a final divorce. This too could change soon if the AIMPLB affidavit in the Shayara Bano case is a sign of things to come.

The situation is similar to that at the Jamia Riyazul Uloom in Old Delhi. The age-old madrasa, built in 1888, is situated opposite the historic Jama Masjid. It has received cases of divorce for more than a century, with a lull being reported only during the Partition. It also gets roughly twenty cases of instant triple talaq a month. It has never received a complaint where a woman has been divorced over a text or WhatsApp message, or even through Facebook or Skype chat. However, much before the Supreme Court judgment in the Shayara Bano case, the madrasa had been considering instant triple talaq to be a single, revocable divorce. Again, here too, the men approach the madrasa more often than the women—though there has been a significant number of women litigants too in recent years—with instances of instant triple talaq. In most cases, the men look for reconciliation after 'talaq, talaq, talaq'. With the wife in agreement, instant triple talaq in such cases is easily considered a revocable divorce and they are allowed to resume cohabitation. The madrasa has a board of clerics qualified to give judgment in such cases. Where the husband and wife both want separation, the board goes by the most preferred way of divorce. Like with the Nagpada outlet, Jamia Riyazul Uloom advises the couple to calm down and talk to each other. It then involves family members to iron out differences. If all attempts fail, the man is allowed to give a single divorce, which he can revoke within the three-month iddat period, failing which, the divorce is effected. All efforts are made to find a solution to avoid repeated visits to other courts; the idea is to provide justice in a given time frame with no expenditure on a lawyer, etc.

Interestingly, most litigants here come from the lower social strata. It receives far fewer cases of khula, a pointer probably to the lack of awareness about women's rights in Islam. The 'two to three cases a month on an average' of khula are usually easier to settle. If the qazi is convinced that the woman is serious about parting ways, khula is effected immediately and the husband is asked to release the woman from wedlock. Most men agree to khula; in case they don't, they are either brought around through negotiation or the wife is advised to give something in return, that is, a part of her mahr, if already paid. Only in rare cases does the husband want to harass the woman. In that case, the family elders are persuaded to prevail upon him to not delay things as khula is considered a woman's unilateral right to divorce by the qazis here and in other madrasas in Delhi, like those in Ajmeri Gate, Seelampur, Babarpur, Mandawali and Inderlok.

While the Nagpada Darul Qaza and Jamia Riyazul Uloom get to settle cases of talaq on a fairly regular basis, the situation is remarkably different in Patna's Imarat Shariah. The Imarat gets cases from Bihar, Jharkhand, Odisha and West Bengal. It, however, gets many times more cases of khula than instant triple talaq. Almost all litigants at the Imarat are Sunnis. It gets only around 300 cases of divorce initiated by men, while as many as 3000 cases every year are that of khula. Interestingly, in more than 95 per cent of cases, khula is granted almost immediately. Further, a whopping 90 per cent–plus women go on to marry another man within a year. This does point to greater awareness among women in that part of the country. What it probably conceals is that when the men pronounce talaq, they do not necessarily come to Imarat Shariah qazis for a second opinion.

The situation is somewhat different at Kithore's Jama Masjid in Uttar Pradesh's Meerut district. The area has a predominance of Sunni Muslims, with around thirty masjids and seven madrasas. At Kithore's Jama Masjid, a talaq case crops up only once in two months, and khula cases almost never. In the rare case of khula, the complainant is directed to Darul Uloom, Deoband. The masjid's imam goes by the most preferred way of divorce, talaq-e-ahsan, and takes pains to point out that one does not have to take recourse to sinful ways when the method approved by the Prophet is available. Here, the Hadith is almost as often quoted as the Quran in coming to a judgment. Interestingly, since the Supreme Court judgment, complaints of instant triple talaq have come down in the locality.

The picture is repeated at Madrasa Islamia Arabia in Muzaffarnagar district in western Uttar Pradesh. The madrasa rarely takes a call on instant triple talaq. Most are referred to Deoband. In days gone by, the occasional case of divorce was handled at the local level itself, with the maulanas ruling in favour of instant triple talaq being the final divorce. Since the Supreme Court judgment, however, a handful of queries have been deflected with replies like 'It is a question of jurisprudence. Let a qazi handle this.'

At Ashraful Madaris in Hardoi, the response is similar. The clerics here too prefer caution on the pronouncement of talaq. When faced with the case of a couple seeking reunion after the pronouncement of instant triple talaq, the madrasa refers them to Nadwatul Uloom, Nadwa, in Lucknow. Similarly, there is 'on an average one case a month' presented at Masjid Bhorgarh in Amethi. In a case of instant triple talaq, the ruling is always in favour of regarding it as a single, revocable divorce. This was one of the rare masjids that launched a campaign against the pronouncement of instant triple talaq and managed to get 300 signatories on board in the run-up to the Supreme Court hearing in May 2017.

The findings from these Darul Qazas and madrasas point to one thing: instant triple talaq is not the monster it is projected to be. Yes, there are cases where insensitive, temperamental, ignorant, even licentious husbands pronounce instant triple talaq to end their marriages, but the percentage of such cases in comparison to the total number of talaq cases is much lower than assumed. The percentage of divorce itself among the community is low, as proved by the Census 2011. Even making an allocation for the possibility that most divorce instances would not be reported in a district or high court, the figures from Darul Qaza and other madrasas point towards a lower divorce rate than often projected by the media. This was also revealed by legal expert Faizan Mustafa, vice chancellor, NALSAR University of Law, Hyderabad. In a May 2017 interview to Scroll.in, he said, 'As per the 2011 census, only 0.49 per cent Muslim women were divorcées.' It is open to reason that not all of them were divorced through the instant triple talaq method; many would have opted for khula or talaq-e-tafweez or mubaraat, etc., besides talaq-e-ahsan and talaq-e-hasan.

Prof. Mustafa collected data from Darul Ifta (institutions that issue fatwas). The data from these institutions in ten states revealed that during 2016–17, as many as 3,40,206 fatwas were sought. Of these, only 6.5 per cent were for triple divorce. On the same issue, husband, wife, relatives and friends sought opinions, meaning that 6.5 per cent was not the rate of triple divorce.

He collected data from seventy-four sharia courts (Darul Qaza) run by the AIMPLB in fifteen states. He found that the sharia courts rarely granted triple divorce, and that divorce was permitted only through one pronouncement, preceded by efforts of reconciliation through arbitration. The triple-talaq rate was as low as 1.28 per cent. Of 1252 divorce cases, only sixteen were of triple divorce.

The BMMA, one of the respondents in the Supreme Court in the Shayara Bano case, conducted its own all-India survey, 'Seeking Justice Within Family—A National Study on Muslim Women's Views on Reforms in Muslim Personal Law'. The survey was conducted in Rajasthan, Gujarat, Maharashtra, Madhya Pradesh, Jharkhand, Bihar, Odisha, Karnataka and Tamil Nadu. As part of the study, 4710 women were surveyed, the purpose of the study being to ascertain the status of Muslim women pertaining to matters of marriage, divorce, maintenance, custody of children, etc. The respondents were above eighteen years of age. Most were from the economically weaker sections, with family incomes of Rs 50,000 or less. The data was collected over six months, from July to December 2013.

As per its findings, of the 525 divorced women, 65.9 per cent were divorced orally, 7.6 per cent through a letter, 3.4 per cent on the phone, three women via email and one via SMS. An overwhelming 88 per cent preferred the talaq-e-ahsan method spread across ninety days as a way of divorce. Interestingly, the BMMA also found that a vast majority of women do not go to the courts, or even to local qazis, and as many as 44 per cent had not received any mahr.

What these findings collectively reveal is that incidents of instant triple talaq are not an insurmountable barrier in the journey towards a more equitable relationship between a Muslim husband and wife. Such instances are few and far between. And arbitration councils like the Darul Qaza, and even some of the more enlightened madrasas, play a positive role in preventing divorce. What they reveal, equally crucially, is that women are beginning to speak up for their rights. As learnt through the Jamia Riyazul Uloom, buttressed by Prof. Mustafa's findings, more and more women are now approaching these arbitration fora because they are both accessible and enjoy a certain degree of acceptance within the community. They are cost-effective and definitely less time-consuming. More such courts might just help in bringing down the rate of divorce further. Of course, ruling out instant triple talaq can be a fine beginning. Campaigns against instant triple talaq, such as the one run by Amethi's Masjid Bhorgarh, are a beacon of hope.

Conclusion

The Way Forward

In less than twenty-four hours after the Supreme Court set aside instant triple talaq, Jharkhand's Fatima Suraiya was divorced by her husband through instant triple talaq. Without ever having got a hint that instant divorce was coming her way, the twenty-seven-year-old resident of Hazaribagh was thrown out of her home along with her daughter. The words 'talaq, talaq, talaq', spoken in anger, were sufficient to end her marriage. Her attempt to get help from the local clerics only resulted in the latter asking for a period of about twenty days before they could come to a conclusion!

Less than a month later, in Jodhpur, a woman called Afsana was divorced by her husband over the phone. Munna, her husband of eight years, divorced her on 18 September 2017. Two days later, he married another woman.

A few days later, in Rajkot, twenty-three-year-old Rubina Lakhani complained to the police that she had been thrashed to unconsciousness by her husband, Afzal. Then he pronounced 'talaq, talaq, talaq'. The woman got to know of the divorce—completely against Islamic procedure—when she came to her senses. She was then thrown out of the house by her husband and his family members, claiming that she had been divorced. The man was booked by the police.

The three incidents do not merely prove the limitations of a judicial order in a society where ignorance renders the best of laws ineffective. They relate a story of local maulanas unable to give the right advice at the right time, and men and women, even educated ones, not sure of their rights and duties in Islam. It is drilled into almost every other man that instant triple talaq is the best, or maybe the only, way to end a marriage. And the maulanas seldom rise to the occasion to save a marriage. The incidents also speak eloquently of the failure of Muslim society to instil in its men the teachings of the Quran; instead, they end up relying on the Quran's interpretation by local maulanas.

The reasons are to be found as much in our patriarchal society as in people's complete ignorance of the Quran. Most common Muslim families in small-town India depend on the local imam to interpret the Quran for them, or even advise them on any issue pertaining to religion. It is not uncommon to see men seeking out an imam or a maulana to calculate *zakat*, which is usually paid in the month of Ramzan. Every year, the questions are the same: is it 2.5 per cent of my earnings or savings? Do I count all my property, including the house I am living in?

And what about the car? Also, do I have to give zakat for my wife? Every year, the imam or the maulana answers by rote, even when answering matters of marriage and divorce. Then people ask, 'Should the marriage take place when the moon is in the ascendance?' or 'Is marriage disallowed in the entire month of Muharram or only in the first ten days?'

Unfortunately, the local imams are often not well versed with the Quran. Probably all of them are hafiz, that is, they have memorized the Quran from the first surah, Fateha, to the last surah, Naas. But they know not what they read or recite. They have no knowledge of Arabic or of Arab society at the time of the revelation of the Quran. Hence, they read the Quran, even commit it to memory, without understanding it. It would probably be the only instance across the world where a book of around 6000 verses and 114 surahs across thirty chapters is memorized by millions without their understanding a sentence. Worse, most of these imams are not reliably conversant with the Hadith either. They usually come from poor families and join a madrasa at least partly because it offers affordable-to-free food and accommodation. This supposedly free accommodation is usually nothing more than a floor to sleep on and two simple meals.

At the first stage in the madrasa, they learn to read the alphabet and join letters to form words before going on to read the Quran. This, in turn, is succeeded by memorizing sessions under a senior maulana. Mistakes in recitation are often met with physical punishment. Once these boys are able to memorize the Quran, with a little ceremony held in the Islamic month of Shaban they leave the madrasa as the prospect of earning Rs 8000 to 12000 a month is too attractive to ignore or delay acceptance.

The madrasas usually impart knowledge of the root words of the Quran, the circumstances of the revelation of each surah, etc., and also the knowledge of the authentic Hadith, but only at a later stage. In the first five years, only the Quran is memorized. There is *tarjuma* (translation), which is taught at a place like Darul Uloom, Deoband, but not in most smaller madrasas. It is only in the sixth year at the madrasa that *tafsir* (commentary) of the Quran is taught. Soon after, the students get to read Ibn Kasir. Much before that, most needy boys step out as hafiz, all keen to start their careers as imams in a nondescript masjid on a paltry salary, with nothing like paid leave, gratuity or medical compensation, etc. The only free thing that comes their way is a Thursday meal offered by a benevolent local, or a little token offered at the end of *taraweeh* prayers during Ramzan. If, in their years at the madrasa, nobody taught them to reason, to explore, to ask questions, as professionals, they neither have the resources nor the opportunity to attain higher knowledge.

These hafiz boys become imams in smaller towns and villages across India, particularly in the Hindi-speaking belt. They recite with perfect diction, their voices well-trained. Unfortunately, they know not what they recite. Hence, when a local resident comes to them for advice, they are not always able to give an informed opinion. Their ignorance often impedes the community's development. There have been instances of imams in areas populated by the poorer sections advising the residents to withdraw their children from public schools if they want them to grow up to be alims! It does not strike them that the first word revealed to the Prophet was 'Iqra', which means 'read', and that Islam makes seeking knowledge the duty of every being, with one verse in the Quran saying, 'Oh Lord! Increase me in knowledge.'

In a case of talaq, the situation can have particularly dire consequences. Despite being hafiz, they are not well versed with the chapters pertaining to different kinds of divorce. As part of a patriarchal society, they would have only heard that three pronouncements of divorce mean that a marriage is over. Nobody at home or at the madrasa tells them that there is a process of effecting a divorce clearly outlined in the Quran. Thus, when the father of a woman approaches the imam for advice after his daughter has received triple talaq through a letter or a text message, the imam is not able to say that this form of divorce is invalid, or to substantiate his argument with verses from the Quran. Some responsible ones merely direct the aggrieved to Deoband or Lucknow, which, again, are often beyond the reach of the poor.

The ignorance of the local imam or maulana often has disastrous consequences for many marriages. In this context, it is important to remember that the main petitioner in the Supreme Court, Shayara Bano, claimed that nobody told her that her marriage subsisted after receiving triple talaq through the post. And no maulana told her about the option of khula being open to a woman to end an unhappy marriage. A well-informed maulana in Allahabad, her husband's residential town, or a caring one in Kashipur, her ancestral place, could have saved her much agony, perhaps even her marriage, and those of Afsana in Jodhpur and Fatima Suraiya in Hazaribagh.

However, it is not just maulanas or local imams in small mosques who are accountable. The rot runs deeper. There is ignorance, at times even opposition, to understanding the Quran. In most Muslim households, when a child starts going to school, his Islamic education also starts at home or at a madrasa nearby. To term it 'Islamic education', though, would be an overstatement. The child begins to learn the Arabic alphabet. Once he is able to join the letters well enough, he starts reading the Quran under a maulana. Since the last chapter of the Quran contains the smallest surahs, often recited in compulsory prayers, the maulanas start the child's tuition with this section. From one chapter to the next, to the next, the child reads them all. Unfortunately, reading is all he does. He does not understand a sentence of what he reads. The maulana teaches him the right diction, the right sound for a 'noon' and a 'quaf', but never is the child told the meaning of any surah or verse. As a result, he grows up like his teachers: reading the Quran but unaware of its meaning.

As an adult, when faced with a problem at home or in the office, such a man is not able to consult the Quran, simply because he never comprehended its meaning, never understood that the solution to his problems lay in the book, not outside. The problem is compounded by the fact that the same man is imparted no knowledge of the authentic Hadith. It is not uncommon to come across educated households with no commentaries of the Quran to be consulted in times of need, or even copies of the authentic Hadith, like Bukhari or Sahi Muslim, etc. This inherited aversion to seeking knowledge is passed on to the next generation. When this man goes to the local mosque, all he hears is a sermon in Arabic. He understands it not. He sits there out of reverence. Occasionally, when there is a Hadith related in a little chat after prayers, no reference is made to its book. Is it authentic? Or is it *zaif* or weak? No maulana ever tells him to consult Bukhari or Sahi Muslim or Daud for reliable Hadith. The wheel of ignorance rolls on.

Thus, when this man, probably as the father of two kids, develops issues with his wife, he has nobody to turn to for the right advice. The same goes for his wife. In the case of at least three of the five petitioners in the Supreme Court, the husband and his family harassed the woman for more dowry. In one case, the things that came as part of the dowry did not meet the expectations of the in-laws. In another case, a car was demanded after marriage.

None of these problems would have been allowed to linger, with a solution being found one way or the other, if these men or their local clerics had consulted the Quran or the Hadith. There is zero tolerance towards dowry in Islam. In fact, it is considered a sin to ask the bride's father to host the wedding feast. The best wedding is the one in which the least expenditure is incurred. Yet,

most maulanas are not able to recite these Hadiths or
quote the best-known preachers on the subject, like Dr
Israr Ahmed or Tariq Jameel or Bilal Philips. All that
they offer the aggrieved women are hollow words of
consolation.

They never, ever, pull up an errant husband, or even
suggest that the woman can leave such a man through khula,
a woman's inalienable right to divorce, where she is not
even expected to disclose the reasons for her decision. The
reality is that most clerics do not know about khula, about
ila, about lian or mubaraat. If they did, Atiya Sabri could
have ended her marriage following the filthy allegations
levelled against her by her husband. Her husband, however,
is unlikely to have read about the circumstances of the
revelation of Surah Nur in the Quran. A man who would
have read the meaning of Surah Nur would have thought
many times over before casting aspersions on the character
of any woman, least of all his wife. The surah was revealed
against the backdrop of a slander campaign launched
against the Prophet's wife, Aisha. Islamic scholar Abul Ala
Mawdudi has dealt with the incident in great detail in his
commentary of the Quran, wherein he reproduces Aisha's
account. She said:

> It was the practice of the Prophet (peace be upon
> him) to decide which of his wives would accompany
> him on a journey by drawing lots. For the expedition
> of Banu al-Mustaliq, the lot fell in my name and so
> I accompanied him. On our return, while we were
> camping at Madina, the Prophet (peace be upon him)

camped for the night at a place. Some time before dawn, preparations were made to set out. I had gone to attend the call of nature and as I was about to return to the camp, my necklace broke and fell down somewhere. I started to look around for it. Meanwhile, the caravan proceeded.

She was left behind and lay there, covered in a sheet, waiting for somebody from the caravan to notice her absence. When the morning arrived, Safwan ibn Muattal al Salami, who was in the habit of sleeping late, took note of her. He was one of the companions of the Prophet during the Battle of Badar. He halted his camel, lowered it for the Prophet's wife to ride, and himself decided to walk the camel. When she rejoined the caravan around noon, it gave rise to a slander campaign, with Ab Allah ibn Ubayy taking the lead role. When the Prophet got to know of this vicious propaganda, he stood by his wife, saying, 'By God, I have never seen anything bad in my wife nor in the person who is subjected to slander and calumny; he is a person who has never visited my house in my absence.'

Further, husbands like Munna, Wajid or Afzal would not have done what they did if they knew Islam. The truth is, despite offering Friday prayers regularly, and sometimes even the five daily prayers, they do not know anything about the rights and responsibilities of a husband in Islam. Else, Munna would have understood that he had no right to pronounce talaq over the phone. So would Ishrat Jahan's husband.

Wajid would have understood the grave significance of putting forth serious allegations without a shred of evidence. The Quran is very particular about safeguarding a woman's honour. A person is required to produce four witnesses if they dare to cast aspersions on a woman's character. Atiya could have been saved the ignominy if her husband had been better aware of the Quran.

As for Afzal, who pronounced divorce while his wife was unconscious, he obviously didn't know that the Quran does not hold such a divorce valid, where a man is in a state of extreme rage—as Afzal was when he thrashed his wife till she fainted—or the partner is unconscious. The Quran states that husband and wife are like garments unto each other. Men such as Afzal and others could have been saved the sin had they known their limits. And their wives' honour could have been saved had the women or the men been aware of the complete picture. Ignorance is all-pervasive. Add to that the fact that these men are usually drunk on notions of male hegemony.

It is this mindset that sees men exclude women from masjids. Never mind that in every azan (call for prayer) they announce, 'Come for prayers, come for success.' Such is their indoctrination that it never strikes them that an azan is heard as often by a woman as a man. Just as a man is supposed to respond to azan by heading to the masjid for prayers, a woman can and should be able to do likewise. Forgotten is the Hadith wherein the Prophet himself said that the best prayer for a man is in the first row, and that for a woman is in the last row. The Prophet stood for segregation of the sexes, not exclusion of women.

Today, most mosques in India, except those maintained by the Ahl-e-Hadith, and occasionally the Jamaat-e-Islami, have no provision for the entry or exit of women, their prayer room or space, etc. Mosques are reduced to a male domain. Women, if they do enter, are considered aliens, another species, who have perchance entered the wrong place.

Until this ignorance of women's rights is dispelled, the Supreme Court order or even a legislation will be adhered to more as the exception than the norm. Like the ban on the caste system, like the prohibition on dowry, the latest court order and a piece of legislation on setting aside instant triple talaq and imprisoning the husband will need social support for it to be effective. And for society to know what is right from what is wrong, it is crucial that the maulanas understand the Quran. They learn the Quran by rote, whereas it encourages man to think, to reason, and to ponder. Surah Muhammad, verse 24, says, 'Then do they not reflect upon the Qur'an, or are there locks upon (their) hearts?'

It is equally crucial for women to know their rights. The Quran, while expecting them to be generous and obedient towards their husbands, also gives them clear rights. It does not expect them to put up with marital cruelty or any demand for dowry, or even for a male heir. It safeguards a woman's income. It makes it incumbent on her to pay her own zakat. It gives her the same reward for a fast or a *salaat* (prayer). Wherever the Quran talks of believing men, it talks of believing women; when it talks of an adulteress, it talks of an adulterer too.

It is for women to understand that if they are trapped in a violent or abusive marriage, they have the right to render such a marriage null and void, either through khula or talaq-e-tafweez or lian. The clause of talaq-e-tafweez needs to be added to the nikahnama to prevent instances of sustained torture of women. In the same way, instant triple talaq needs to be ruled out through the nikahnama itself, as the AIMPLB said in its affidavit in the Supreme Court.

Similarly, for a husband, it is vital to know his responsibilities. He is not supposed to receive any dowry— the Prophet gave no dowry to any of his daughters. Nor did he receive it from any of his fathers-in-law. A man is supposed to pay mahr at the time of the wedding and maintain his wife to the best of his resources. He is not allowed to bring another woman home, even as a legally married wife, without the permission of his first wife. And in case of a final divorce, Islam does not ask a woman to do a halala to come back to her husband. She should not have to pay for his error. Halala, the way it operates in our country, is a mockery of the right to self-determination Islam confers on a woman.

Yes, the way forward lies in a better understanding of the Quran. No judgment of the Supreme Court has gone against the Quran. The legal requirements of a successful marriage are the same as expected in Islam. It's time somebody started a crash course in understanding the Quran for many maulanas. And a weekend one for most husbands and wives. It is about time we reflected upon the teachings of the Quran, as told through Surah Muhammad, named after the man who said that the best of men is the one who is the best to his wife.

Sources

Chapter 1: 'Like Garments unto Each Other'

1. *The Glorious Quran* (Surah Baqarah, Surah Rum, Surah Nur), Arabic original.
2. *Hadith Tirmidhi* (New Delhi: Markazi Maktaba Islami, 1988).
3. *Hadith Bukhari* (New Delhi: Markazi Maktaba Islami, 1988).
4. Maulana Wahiduddin Khan, *Concerning Divorce* (New Delhi: Goodword Books, 2001).
5. Abdullah Yusuf Ali, trans. *The Quran* (Amana Publications, 1934).
6. Mufti Abdul Dayam Jalali and Qazi Mohammed Sanaullah Usmani, *Tafsir-e-Mazhar* (Karachi: Darul Ishaat, 1999).
7. At-Tabari, *Jami al-Bayan* (1966).

Chapter 2: As the Quran Says It

1. Prof. Syed Vickar Ahmed, English trans. *The Quran* (USA: Book of Signs Foundation, 2005), translation approval, Cairo: Al-Azhar University.

2. Maulana Wahiduddin Khan and Dr Farida Khanum, English trans. *The Quran* (New Delhi: Goodword Books, 2016).
3. *The Glorious Quran* (Surah Baqarah, Surah Nisa, Surah Ahzaab, Surah Mujadila, Surah Talaq), Arabic original.
4. Abdullah Yusuf Ali, trans. *The Quran* (USA: Amana Publications, 1934).
5. Maulana Abul Ala Mawdudi, *Towards Understanding the Quran* (New Delhi: Markazi Maktaba Islami, 1994).
6. Mufti Abdul Dayam Jalali and Qazi Mohammed Sanaullah Usmani, *Tafsir-e-Mazhari* (Karachi: Darul Ishaat, 1999).

Chapter 3: Till Talaq Do Us Part

1. *The Glorious Quran* (Surah Baqarah, Surah Ahzaab, Surah Ta Ha), Arabic original.
2. *Bukhari Sharief* (New Delhi: Markazi Maktaba Islami, 1988).
3. Tahir Mahmood, *Muslim Law in India and Abroad* (New Delhi: Universal Law Publishing, 2012).
4. Mohammed Hasnain Haykel, *Hazrat Umar: Farooq-e-Azam* (Delhi: Islamic Books Foundation, 2004).
5. *Hadith Tirmidhi* (New Delhi: Markazi Maktaba Islami, 1988).
6. Mufti Abdul Dayam Jalali, Urdu trans. *Sahi Muslim Sharief* (Delhi: Farid Book Depot, 2014).

Chapter 4: Different Schools of Sunni Thought

1. Mufti Abdul Dayam Jalali and Qazi Mohammed Sanaullah Usmani, *Tafsir-e-Mazhari* (Karachi: Darul Ishaat, 1999).
2. Imam Abu Hanifa, *Al-Fiqah Ul Akbar* (Riyadh: 1981).
3. Prof. Furqan Ahmad, *Triple Talaq: An Analytical Study with Emphasis on Socio-Legal Aspects* (New Delhi: Regency Publications, 2002).
4. Imam Malik, *Kitab al Talaq*.
5. *Ithna Ashar.*

Chapter 5: Halala: A Mischievous Interpretation

1. *The Glorious Quran*, Arabic original.
2. Mufti Abdul Dayam Jalali, Urdu trans., *Sahi Muslim Sharief* (Delhi: Farid Book Depot, 2014).
3. *Bukhari Sharief* (New Delhi: Markazi Maktaba Islami, 1988).

Chapter 6: The Quran on Polygamy

1. Prof. Syed Vickar Ahmed, English trans. *The Quran* (USA: Book of Signs Foundation, 2005), translation approval, Cairo: Al-Azhar University.
2. Kauser Edappagath, *Divorce and Gender Equity in Muslim Personal Law of India* (Gurgaon: LexisNexis, 2014).
3. *Tafsir Ibn Kasir* (Muzaffarnagar: Idara Dawat ul Quran, 1994).
4. Maulana Abul Ala Mawdudi, *Towards Understanding the Quran* (New Delhi: Markazi Maktaba Islami, 1994).
5. *Bukhari Sharief* (New Delhi: Markazi Maktaba Islami, 1988).

Chapter 7: Khula: A Woman's Right to Divorce

1. *The Glorious Quran* (Surah Baqarah).
2. Maulana Wahiduddin Khan, *Concerning Divorce* (New Delhi: Goodword Books, 2001).
3. *Hadith Tirmidhi* (New Delhi: Markazi Maktaba Islami, 1988).
4. Maulana Muhammed Ali, translation of the Quran.
5. Maulana Abul Ala Mawdudi, *Huquq al Zawjain* (New Delhi: Markazi Maktaba Islami, 1988).
6. Kauser Edappagath, *Divorce and Gender Equity in Muslim Personal Law of India* (Gurgaon: LexisNexis, 2014).

Chapter 8: Other Ways for Her . . .

1. *The Glorious Quran*, Arabic original.
2. Maulana Wahiduddin Khan, *Concerning Divorce* (New Delhi: Goodword Books, 2001).
3. Maulana Wahiduddin Khan (edited), *Al-Risala* (New Delhi: 1993).
4. Kauser Edappagath, *Divorce and Gender Equity in Muslim Personal Law of India* (Gurgaon: LexisNexis, 2014).

Chapter 9: Divorce Methods of the Shias

1. *The Glorious Quran*, Arabic original.
2. Mufti Abdul Dayam Jalali, Urdu trans. *Sahi Muslim Sharief* (Delhi: Farid Book Depot, 2014).
3. Imam Khumainei, *Tauzih-ul-Masail* (1966).

Chapter 10: Divorce during the Mughal Age

1. Interview with Prof. Shireen Mustafa (2017).
2. Abdul Qadir Badayuni, *Muntakhab ul Tawarikh*, Urdu trans. by Abdur Rehman Dehlavi (New Delhi: Akif Publishers, 1981).

Chapter 11: The Supreme Court's *Shayara Bano vs the Union of India and Others* Judgment

1. The Supreme Court's judgment report in the *Shayara Bano vs the Union of India and Others* case.

Chapter 12: The Women behind the Change

1. Interview with Zakia Soman (2017).
2. Interview with Noorjehan Safia Niaz (2017).
3. Interview with Shayara Bano (2017).

4.   Interview with Gulshan Parveen's brother (2017).
5.   Interview with Aafreen Rehman's cousin sister (2017).
6.   Interview with Atiya Sabri (2017).
7.   Interview with Ishrat Jahan (2017, 2018).

Chapter 13: Rulings That Paved the Way

1.   Kauser Edappagath, *Divorce and Gender Equity in Muslim Personal Law of India*, (Gurgaon: LexisNexis, 2014).

Chapter 14: AIMPLB's Points of Action

1.   The AIMPLB's submissions before the Supreme Court.
2.   The AIMPLB's press release on the Shayara Bano case (September 2017).

Chapter 15: No to Instant Talaq in Muslim Countries

1.   Maulana Wahiduddin Khan, *Concerning Divorce* (New Delhi: Goodword Books, 2001).
2.   Tahir Mahmood, *Muslim Law in India and Abroad* (New Delhi: Universal Law Publishing, 2012).
3.   The Supreme Court's judgment report in the *Shayara Bano vs the Union of India and Others* case.

Chapter 16: Instant Triple Talaq and Khula in Qazi Courts

1.   Interview with the rector of Jamia Riyazul Uloom (Delhi: 2017).
2.   Interview with the imam of Jama Masjid, Kithore, 2017.
3.   Interview with the imam of Madrasa Islamia Arabia, 2017.
4.   Interview with the media in-charge of Imarat Shariah, Patna, 2017.

5. Interview with Abdul Azim, spiritual healer in Mumbai, 2017.
6. Interview with the imam of Ashraful Madaris, Hardoi, 2017.
7. Interview with the imam of Masjid Bhorgarh, Amethi, 2017.
8. Prof. Faizan Mustafa interview with *Scroll* (May 2017), 2017.
9. Bharatiya Muslim Mahila Andolan's all-India survey on divorce, 2017.

Conclusion: The Way Forward

1. Maulana Abul Ala Mawdudi, *Towards Understanding the Quran* (New Delhi: Markazi Maktaba Islami, 1994).
2. *Daud Sharief* (Delhi: Farid Book Depot, 1999).